MW00560144

HOUSES THAT CAN SAVE THE WORLD

HOUSE

COURTENAY SMITH

CAN

THE W

S THAT

SAVE

SEAN TOPHAM

ORLD

CONTENTS

INTRODUCTION
We are all architects

Can houses save the world? We believe they can, when we all come together to build them more sustainably. And for those who may be undecided about jumping on board, we offer this thought: changing the way our homes are constructed could help alleviate many of the world's problems, instead of making them worse. Within these pages, we present a collection of buildings that demand big changes to the way we imagine and build our homes today.

We are not architects. We are not designers, engineers or builders. We are two curious homeowners with a belief in the power of imagination to make life better. Our curiosity got us talking with architects, researchers, self-builders, designers and others who are embracing the challenges facing the human race with strategies that are direct, original and often surprisingly simple. Participatory and mindful, these new homebuilding tactics link together knowledge and methods from myriad fields, including architecture, art, design, philosophy, psychology, computer science, chemistry, microbiology and many more to create innovative and sustainable homes for future generations.

Researching this book has given us hope. We have found that nothing short of a global design revolution is underway, as inventive people around the world tackle issues ranging from climate change to environmental degradation and depletion of resources; global migration to expanding cities, aging populations and new definitions of family; poverty to excess waste and pollution. As useful and vernacular responses to tough challenges, the strategies presented here stem from a variety of international circumstances that influence the way we view the place we call 'home'.

The heroes spearheading this revolution are part of a worldwide movement of empathetic housebuilding that relies on considering things from multiple perspectives, rather than accepting top-down design processes or end products delivered by so-called experts or developers. They come from different parts of the world, have different fields of expertise and face different challenges, but they share a common goal as initiators, collaborators and partners in taking action to make their homes and the world a better place. In our Anthropocene era, where human activity is the dominant influence on the environment, *Houses That Can Save the World* points to an optimistic trend for networked problem-solving and perseverance. Changing the way we build our homes can produce a brighter future.

We say 'heroes', because many of these individuals have had to overcome extraordinary obstacles to do something different. When we began our research, it quickly became apparent that 'different' is often synonymous with 'difficult'. Moving away from standard materials, techniques or living arrangements typically means push-back in the form of zoning restrictions, denial of permission permits and expensive land rights, as well as increases in costs and time. Many of the projects took years to realize. But what has become clear is that the more these ideas become second nature, become 'normal', the more they make a difference.

We find homes fascinating because they are common to us all and serve as the building blocks of our communities, towns and cities. A global tipping point in favour of sustainable living can proceed from small changes at the personal level. We have included over 150 international examples, representing a wide range of incomes and tastes, and demonstrating that a shift in personal practice does not have to mean a loss of individuality. Indeed, we have been positively surprised by the fact that these new ideas are taking root across cultural and economic brackets. It's a refreshingly broad mix, which we've divided into overarching strategies, with each revealing a part of the bigger picture by telling the stories of the key projects and the people behind them.

From wholly new techniques to creative reuse of existing buildings and materials, the strategies included here demonstrate how, with openness and awareness, designers and builders are experimenting with the home as a unit to address some of the biggest problems facing the world today. It's not a scientific study or a formal evaluation of the impact each project might have, but rather a collection of inspirational ideas that we wish were more widely available to anyone who wants to make a difference.

Intended as an inspirational sourcebook for anyone interested in building or adapting their home, *Houses That Can Save the World* is also a soft manifesto and gentle reminder that lots of small changes can add up to make a big difference. For anyone who is committed to preserving the planet for future generations – and dreaming of their own version of a house that could save the world – this is a book that can be turned to for impetus and reflection.

ASSIMILATE

ASSIMILATE
Blending in

To assimilate is to be modest and humble, mindful of one's surroundings, and to integrate into a place by coexisting with it. The homes in this chapter have been absorbed into their contexts by imitating the natural characteristics at hand. Temperature and climate, flora and fauna, as well as the effects of time are the primary 'materials'. The orientation of the houses on their sites also plays a key role in connecting to these natural energies.

For Ensamble Studio, this is an ongoing conversation. In 2010 the architects built The Truffle (p. 31), a retreat on the Spanish Costa da Morte. They had no preconceived plans, yet were surprised by how earth and concrete exchanged properties to form a camouflaged mass that integrated into its surroundings. Casa Meztitla (p. 32), designed by EDAA, also seamlessly merges with its environment and might be mistaken for an outcropping of the rocky El Tepozteco mountain behind it. The house works in harmony with the temperate climate by recycling all of its own water and giving some back to the site and to the animals who come by for a drink.

In the case of Casa Invisible (p. 26), in Ljubljana, Slovenia, architects Delugan Meissl created an 'invisible' low-carbon prototype with an exterior clad in mirrors, which allows it to disappear into the landscape. The long-term vision for the project was to design a house that was flexible, had minimum impact, and would reflect – literally – its surroundings. The lightweight units and use of local materials ensure that it rests gently on the ground and can be dismantled easily, minimizing its environmental footprint.

For Héctor Barroso, a project will typically begin with making sketches and models that capture in-situ sensations. This method helps translate experience into form, resulting in residences – such as Entre Pinos (p. 24), five weekend houses in Valle de Bravo, Mexico – that are deeply rooted in the land. Built with bricks coated with the red soil excavated for the foundations, the homes exude a down-to-earth authenticity, as though they had always been there. Indeed, Barroso considers timelessness and aging to be valid material properties, ones that will take clients down a longer, quieter path.

Taller Hector Barroso
Entre Pinos Housing, 2017
Valle de Bravo, Mexico

Each of the five houses has a closed
elevation to the north, but is open
to the south, providing views over
the forest. The 30 cm (12 in.)-thick
brick walls are coated in a mud
render, made by mixing soil
excavated for the foundations with
clay and cement. This was then
applied by hand, resulting in a warm
and pulsating glow, inside and out.

ASSIMILATE

TRIAS
Slate Cabin, 2017
Snowdonia, Wales, UK

This writer's retreat on the edge of Snowdonia National Park was inspired by the bedrock of Wales: slate. The architects, therefore, chose to clad the structure with reclaimed slate tiles gathered from nearby farms and marked by weather and time. 'Wales is a unique landscape,' they explain, 'scattered with stone-strewn mountains, abandoned quarries and old slate-covered farmhouses that have stood for hundreds of years' – qualities that encouraged the team to base their design around this locally significant natural resource.[1]

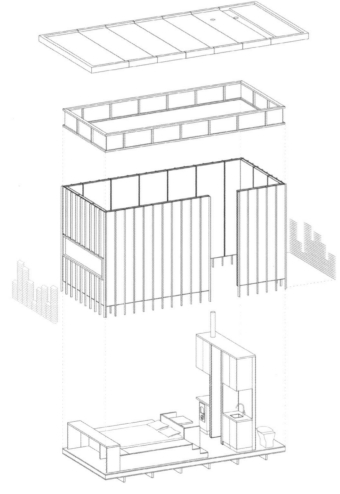

Delugan Meissl
Associated Architects
Casa Invisible, 2013
Ljubljana, Slovenia

The architects believe Casa Invisible, at 50 m² (538 sq ft), to be a long-term solution for medium-sized housing. If more space is needed, expanding the building is easy and efficient, both in terms of energy and materials. One of the biggest challenges the team faced was finding a building company that shared their vision, and would be willing to collaborate and develop the details of the project with a focus on simplicity, sustainability and cost. The team is currently considering releasing it as an open-source design.

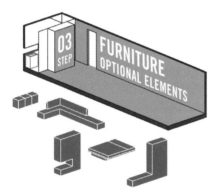

BLENDING IN

Bureau and Leopold Banchini
Antoine, 2014
Verbier, Switzerland

Following Switzerland's long tradition of living and hiding in camouflaged bunkers in the Alps, Antoine is a one-person wooden shelter in the shape of a boulder, perched on a rockfall field below the mountain. Designed by Daniel Zamarbide of Bureau and architect Leopold Banchini, and named after Antoine, the Swiss herdsman who survives a mountain collapse after being buried under a large rock in *Derborence* (1934) by Charles Ferdinand Ramuz, the tiny cabin contains only the very basics for living: a fireplace, bed, table, stool and window.

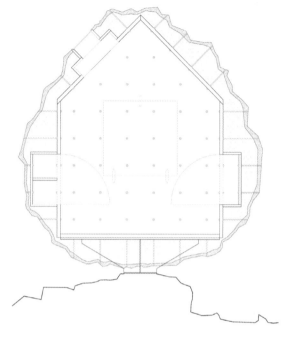

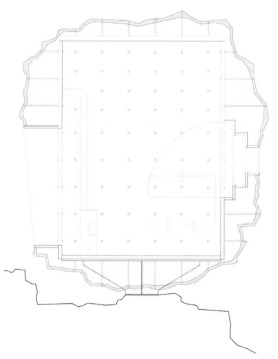

**Gartnerfuglen Arkitekter
and Mariana de Delás
Gjemmested, 2017
Telemark, Norway**

This little hideaway, a collaborative effort between Norwegian firm Gartnerfuglen Arkitekter and Spanish architect Mariana de Delás, was dug into a steep rocky slope facing a mountain lake. When in use, it serves as a fishing cottage and retreat, and is only accessible by boat. The inconvenient site, note the architects, was determined by the desire to retreat, completely isolated from other people, and connect with nature.[2]

The site was dug out by hand, with rocks placed in the water to form a pier for docking. The timber skeleton is clad in birch twigs to camouflage the hut and insulate it by forming a pocket of air. A large picture window reflects the water below; inside, it opens up onto picturesque views of the outdoors. The interior is intimate and divided into a live/work space with a built-in desk and upper-level sleeping area for two people.

**Mary Arnold-Forster Architects
An Cala, 2019
Sutherland, Scotland, UK**

This single-storey house, comprising thirteen individual modules, is situated at the top of Loch Nedd in the Scottish Highlands, in a landscape characterized by empty moorland and woodlands of birch and rowan trees. It is surrounded by the heather, peat and grass that is typical of the area. The exterior is covered with a thin rainscreen cladding of larch, which resembles birchwood in winter.

'My intention was to celebrate this landscape, which is key to the sense of place,' says architect Mary Arnold-Forster. 'We achieved this by lifting the building up off the ground to avoid breaking any rocks at all.'[3]

Ensamble Studio
The Truffle, 2010
Costa da Morte, Spain

This small vacation retreat on the Galician coast of Spain is the result of explorations into a process set into motion, but not controlled, by the architects. Without being certain of the outcome, the team engaged with the materials at hand, placing bales of local hay into the earth and covering them with concrete. After a year, the mound was cut open; the neighbour's calf completed the process by eating the hay inside. The interior space was also not designed, but the result of happy accidents. The soil that surrounded the concrete while it cured gave the material its final texture and colour, while the contours of the space came about through a natural process instigated by human intervention.

EDAA
Casa Meztitla, 2014
Tepoztlán, Mexico

Casa Meztitla, located in Tepoztlán, south of Mexico City, was built from materials that will age naturally and blend into their surroundings: concrete for the foundation, volcanic rock and cement for the walls and white cement and lime for the render. No mains water is needed for the house, as all rainwater filters in, but does not drain away quickly. A covered potable water reservoir lies beneath the grass patio and a large, circular open maintenance reservoir harvests unabsorbed rain and greywater. The swimming pool is filled with reused water.

'Most new housing projects view inhabitation as a very specific situation,' says architect Luis Arturo García. 'But it's your own environment that needs to provide these in the best possible way.'[4]

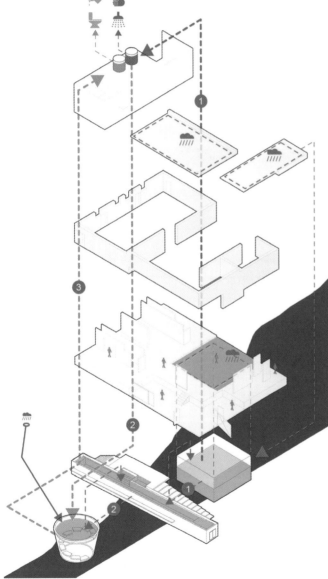

Tatiana Bilbao Estudio
Los Terrenos, 2016
Monterrey, Mexico

In this 480 m² (5,167 sq ft) holiday retreat built on a forested hillside, two buildings containing different living functions are set at opposite corners of the site in an intentional response to the landscape and engagement with the organically shaped pool at the centre.

Clad in mirrored glass, the larger structure seems to dissolve into the trees. It contains a kitchen, living room and dining area, with direct access to the outdoors. The smaller L-shaped structure of clay and rammed earth is set partly below ground level. It houses two bedrooms, facing in opposite directions, with stacked (or terraced) interiors and retractable glass doors.

Reform Architekt
Izabelin House, 2014
Izabelin, Poland

To prevent the home from dominating its site in eastern Poland, the architects clad the lower level of the building with reflective panels. This allows the house to 'disappear' into the forest, with the upper storey appearing to float among the trees.

BREATHE

BREATHE
Plants for people

Plants make us feel good. For those living in an urban landscape dominated by concrete, asphalt and smog, filling your homes with plants, says the Royal Horticultural Society, can lift your mood and reduce stress. For the architects of the projects included here, the relationship between plants, people and their homes is so fundamental that buildings and nature blur into one.

In his House for Trees series (pp. 38–40), Vo Trong Nghia put plants at the centre of his designs, both to help regulate temperatures and to bring people closer to nature. Having grown up in one of the hottest regions of Vietnam, with no electricity, he learned early on the importance of natural ventilation and shade when designing for a hot climate. Bringing nature into the home and playing with the boundaries between inside and out also informed Daita2019 in Tokyo (p. 43). On a trip to the Virunga mountains in Rwanda, Suzuko Yamada had observed gorilla communities in the rainforest. Like the animals' nests in the dense vegetation, his designs have no walls to divide living and outdoor space, but instead a series of windows, walkways, terraces and screens among an array of scaffolding poles, which can be dismantled and reassembled in different configurations.

Stefano Boeri has also made planting the priority with his Vertical Forest prototype in Milan (p. 41), two residential towers planted with 800 trees, 15,000 perennials and 5,000 shrubs. Boeri spent years researching and cultivating the most suitable plants, which are tended by a group of flying gardeners who descend from the rooftop on ropes to assess, prune, remove and replace them. Careful management of the planting is essential to keep the residents happy – people, plants, birds and insects alike. As well as bringing nature into built-up areas, heavily planted homes can also provide a source of food. The Farmhouse (p. 42), designed by Austrian architectural studio Precht, is an attempt to bring city dwellers and agriculture closer together. Their proposal is a prefabricated, modular building system based on the structure of traditional A-frame houses. Modules can be arranged to create anything from a tiny house to an apartment block, all wrapped with vertically stacked gardens.

Vo Trong Nghia Architects
House for Trees, 2014
Ho Chi Minh, Vietnam

With the rapid expansion of the concrete jungles of Vietnam's major cities like Ho Chi Minh and Hanoi, people have begun to see how important it is to bring plants into their homes. The houses shown on these pages are part of a series of homes by Vo Trong Nghia Architects that seek to return greenery to densely populated urban areas. This became especially significant during the Covid-19 pandemic in 2020. The first in the series, House for Trees, comprises five concrete blocks, which serve as giant plant pots for large, tropical trees. Each block has a different use, with a library, dining room, kitchen and altar room on the ground level, and bedrooms and bathrooms above. Linked by open walkways, they surround a small courtyard, which provides a focal point for each tower and blurs the boundary between house and garden. As well as providing growing space, the rooftops act as stormwater basins. Like the other homes in the series, the house has a concrete façade with a bamboo-like texture that softens its appearance.

Vo Trong Nghia Architects
Bamboo House, 2016
Ho Chi Minh, Vietnam

Bamboo House develops the series with a prototype home that borders one of Ho Chi Minh's many narrow alleyways. These lanes, known as *hem*, are 2 to 3 m (7 to 10 ft) wide and usually lined with rows of narrow buildings, giving them the appearance of a ravine. The architects designed the four-storey house for a slim strip sandwiched between a dense row of other properties. The front and back of the building are covered in plants, which helps to keep the house cool and reduces the need for air-conditioning. The client notes that he wakes up to the sound of birds chirping every morning, and that his home feels like a jungle in the middle of a bustling city.

An array of large bamboo planters covers the front façade, forming deep eaves to allow windows to be left open during the rainy season and let air inside. Bamboo is a recurring motif in the house, and the pattern of bamboo poles continues in the moulding of the concrete.

Vo Trong Nghia Architects
Ha House, 2019
Ho Chi Minh, Vietnam

Designed for a slender plot and to house a three-generation family, Ha House is a series of interconnected climbing gardens. The clients wanted a large green garden where children could play and the adults could entertain, along with a swimming pool, space for exercising, a granny annexe, living room and dining room with kitchen, and parking – all on the ground floor. The architects proposed dividing the large garden into a series of smaller, connecting gardens that intertwine with terraces and different parts of the house. The façades of the lower floors gradually step away from the street in a twisting pattern, and sit beneath a cantilevered top floor that juts out to meet the line of neighbouring properties and shelters the areas below. Trees of varying sizes screen the house from the street, filter direct sunlight and cool the air. Gaps created by the irregular pattern of each floor allow daylight and fresh air to pass through the home.

Vo Trong Nghia Architects
Breathing House, 2019
Ho Chi Minh, Vietnam

Like Bamboo House (p. 38), Breathing House is also designed for a narrow plot, only 3.9 m (13 ft) wide, crowded by other buildings and accessed via a small alleyway. A vine-covered steel mesh covers the front, top and rear of the house, offering privacy and filtering direct sunlight. Beneath this 'green veil' sits a staggered, five-storey mix of indoor and outdoor space, topped with a terrace and roof garden. The arrangement of pocket gardens on each floor ventilates the home and floods it with indirect light, giving views of greenery and the sky above from different parts of the house.

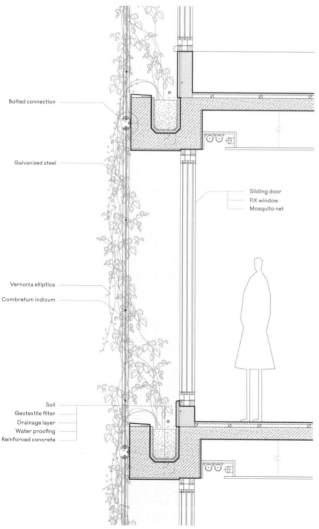

Bolted connection

Galvanized steel

Sliding door
FIX window
Mosquito net

Vernonia elliptica
Combretum indicum

Soil
Geotextile filter
Drainage layer
Water proofing
Reinforced concrete

Stefano Boeri Architetti
Vertical Forest, 2014
Milan, Italy

The first rollout of the Vertical Forest scheme is a pair of towers built on a 3,000 m² (32,000 sq ft) site in the Porta Nuova area of Milan. Each tower provides space that is equivalent to 50,000 m² (538,000 sq ft) of single-family housing, and the same amount of vegetation as 30,000 m² (322,000 sq ft) of woodland. Balconies are staggered across the façade in a pattern that allows for the growth of large trees, even across three floors. The towers are clad in bark-like brown stoneware, giving them the appearance of a pair of gigantic trees, with white used to provide contrast and further highlight the planting. A team of botanists and ethnologists began cultivating the plants in 2010 in a special botanical nursery, readying them for the conditions on the towers. The final planting acts as a filter to produce oxygen and absorb CO_2 and the fine particles produced by traffic, while also acting as a barrier to noise. The plants are monitored digitally, and water is drawn largely from filtered wastewater from the towers.

Precht
The Farmhouse, 2017
Prototype

The Farmhouse is a proposal by Austrian architectural firm Precht for a fully modular, flat-packed building. Wood is the primary construction material, with cross-laminated panels used for the main structure, finishes and planters. The system gives residents a tool for designing their own homes, according to their spatial requirements for living and growing food. Different structural and gardening elements, waste-management units, water treatment, hydroponics and solar systems can also be chosen. Larger homes are assembled as duplex-sized A-frames, with a generous open living space and kitchen on the first floor, and an angled space on the second floor for bedrooms and bathrooms. The sloping walls provide room for gardening on the outside of the building and create a V-shaped buffer zone between the apartments, which also lets in air and light. There are three layers in each wall of the frame: an inside layer for finishes, electricity and pipes; a middle layer for insulation; and a plant-covered outside layer for a water supply.

BREATHE

Precht
Yin and Yang House, 2017
Edersee, Germany

Like The Farmhouse (opposite), Precht's Yin and Yang House aims to bring people closer to food production. Garden space on the tiny rural plot is limited, so planters for vegetables, herbs and fruit were integrated into the design of the stepped roof. Two separate halves of the house – one for living, one for working – are intertwined like a yin and yang symbol, giving the house the look of a valley with hills on either side. The channel in the roof funnels rainwater to the ground, where it can be stored and used to water the plants. According to the architects, the living roof transforms the house over time. From vibrant colours in spring to a white snowfield in winter, the house changes and transforms itself in harmony with its surroundings.

Suzuko Yamada Architects
Daita2019, 2019
Tokyo, Japan

There is no wall as such between this house by Suzuko Yamada Architects and its garden, but rather a composite arrangement of windows with aluminium, wood and steel sashes. By opening and closing these sashes, the house and garden flow into each other and back again.

Having factored in cost, maintenance and the possibility for expansion and reconstruction, Yamada chose a wood frame for the interior and a steel frame for the exterior. The design of a system of pipes that can be easily taken apart and reassembled using clamps means the house can be customized according to the demands of daily life, from changing doorways to adding a balustrade or a washing line, as well as structural elements such as squared timbers and steel pipes. Staircases, window frames, furniture, curtains, potted plants, bicycles, watering cans and shovels, books, DVDs and clothes are all visible, revealing varied scenes from life.

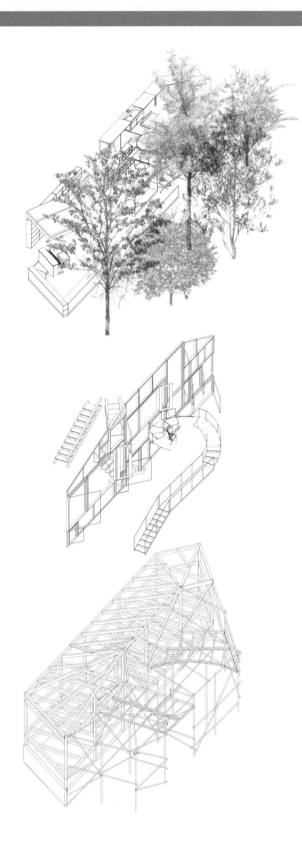

BREATHE

BURROW

BURROW
What if you excavated accommodation?

Burrowing into the ground is an intuitive act. It is also a less invasive method of constructing a home, leaving natural habitats relatively unspoiled, and engages with the site at eye level. On the island of Menorca, Spain, a subterranean habitat emerged from the cast-off shell of a stone quarry (p. 52). Rather than imposing a preconceived vision onto the space, Antón Garcia-Abril and Débora Mesa of Ensamble Studio chose to make a few stone cuts for ventilation and added a water cistern and solar panels. As they see it, it's simply about measuring what actions to take, if any.

David A. Garcia of MAP Architects had a similar approach to discovering living space. His proposal for an Iceberg Living Station (p. 54) aims to house 100 residents with as little construction and environmental impact as possible by carving into an existing iceberg, using the caterpillar excavators already on site. Tunnelling also protects the ecology of a place. Bjarne Mastenbroek of SeARCH and Christian Müller used the method to construct a small retreat in Vals, Switzerland (p. 50), which adapts to the natural incline and preserves the impressive views. The idea, notes Müller, is to let nature lead.

Burrowing also makes good thermal sense, which is why Rama Estudio sited Casa Patios (p. 54) beneath an insulating roof of stones, soil and planting. In Poland, Przemek Olczyk of Mobius Architekci also set Green Line (p. 51) into the natural decline of its site, situating the majority of the volume beneath a green roof. For House in Monsaraz (p. 51) by Portuguese firm Aires Mateus, the solution was to place 80 per cent of the precast wall below ground and cover the roof with soil and plants, leaving the landscape virtually undisturbed.

Design-build firm i/thee, in collaboration with Roundhouse Platform, employed a related approach with Agg Hab (p. 55), a prototype dwelling in Clarendon, Texas. The team dug out two holes and cast them with multiple layers of recycled organic papier-mâché. As soon as the paper shells were dry, they flipped them over and placed them on top of the holes. The paraboloid caps enclose the structures to create habitable space derived from the earth.

**SeARCH and
Christian Müller Architects
Villa Vals, 2009
Vals, Switzerland**

The small village of Vals, with a population of just under 1,000, has the special character of a deep valley that is entered through a narrow space, before opening up to a splendid vista. It not a place of transit, but a destination with a focus on agriculture. With the opening of Peter Zumthor's Thermal Bath in 1996, Vals became known internationally, and the community has since invested in important architectural projects that both enhance a visit to this unique place and enrich the local way of life. Villa Vals can only be accessed by a secluded underground tunnel, which begins in the adjacent barn. The home contributes to a healthy ecology in more ways than one: not only does it peacefully coexist within its surroundings, but it was also constructed from local materials, by local craftsmen, thus keeping the handworker tradition of this particular region alive.

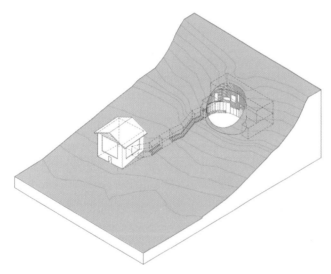

Aires Mateus
House in Monsaraz, 2018
Alentejo, Portugal

The scale of the house is big (174 m², or 1,873 sq ft), but its impact is small. The public areas are all contained within the earth, opening up to a huge domed canopy that extends the space into the landscape. The bedrooms are intimate and look onto small circular patios, whose bright white walls reach up to the roof and provide an uninterrupted view of the sky. Access to the house is from a staircase hidden on the roof, where rows of metal rods serve as the only indications of the home's presence. The construction was very low tech, built by an elderly man and his son out of concrete poured into handmade wooden casts.

'We tend to talk a lot about sustainability from an engineering point of view,' says architect Manuel Aires Mateus. 'These are not our foremost concerns. This house is often described by visitors as the place to see the stars or the place to see the birds. Our concern is being clear and open to transformation. We know this from the Europeans, whose centuries-old buildings are adaptable.'[5]

Mobius Architekci
Green Line, 2019
Warmia, Poland

Embedded into the morphology of the landscape, Green Line was deliberately positioned to take advantage of a natural fold in the landscape. The house's cantilevered roof, covered with vegetation, extends the top ledge of this fold to form a sunken atrium. This not only provides privacy and intimacy, but also helps protect the house from the strong winds that are typical of the region. Materials used for the floors and timber on the façade were all locally sourced.

Ensamble Studio
C'an Terra, 2020
Menorca, Spain

Formerly a sandstone quarry, C'an Terra also served as an ammunition storage during the Spanish Civil War in the 1930s. The industrial history of the cavern is evident in the slices and cuts along its surface. To bring in more daylight, the architects made a few additional cuts and allowed the blocks to simply drop into the space – with one still holding a tree. Translucent curtains help separate private and public areas. A series of cast slabs, made by mixing cement with Marés sandstone, contains the necessary mechanical systems and conforms to the topography of the site. The home can be used off-grid, thanks to solar panels, a water cistern and a septic tank. If architecture can be considered as the transfer of an idea or drawing into a built mass, here the process is reversed: a found object is captured as 3D digital scans, enabling a reinterpretation of the original concept.

Rama Estudio
Casa Patios, 2018
Lasso, Ecuador

Located in Cotopaxi province, this home was commissioned by a family who wanted to enjoy the countryside. The split roof is supported by solid rock walls, which form subterranean tracts that house the private and functional areas of the home. An open and generous social area with floor-to-ceiling windows sits within a large central space, connecting to the two exterior courtyards that give the house its name. All of the interior walls are made from bahareque panels, set into eucalyptus frames (eucalyptus trees were originally brought over from Australia, but now grow in the Ecuadoran tropics). The vernacular building method of bahareque dates back to the Pre-Columbian era, and was used widely in Latin America before industrial methods took hold. The construction material is similar to adobe, and usually consists of clay or mud, reinforced with sticks, cane or bamboo. It is believed to be superior to masonry owing to its durability and thermal and insulating properties. Here, earth from the construction site was used, and the material's natural colour and rough texture gives the interior a calming, natural glow.

MAP Architects
Iceberg Living Station, 2010
Antarctica

The sheer remoteness and wildness of the Antarctic has in recent years lured increasing numbers of adventurers searching for extreme experiences – over 56,000 during the 2018–19 season, according to industry reports, an increase of over 50 per cent from 2014–15. This added strain on the environment could be mitigated by a softer approach to inhabiting its biosphere.

David A. Garcia of MAP Architects proposes carving into an existing tabular iceberg (a flat sheet of ice that has detached from an ice shelf), using the caterpillar excavators already present to clear the snow. Their scooping movement produces a typology of curves that form the interior. Wind generators and solar panels provide all of the necessary energy. The design is both green and community-oriented, with individual sleeping quarters but shared everyday infrastructure, as well as a canteen, kitchen, toilets and conference hall. Food and other perishables can be transported to the site in containers, which, once empty, provide storage for waste and greywater residue.

At the end of the iceberg's life cycle, energy infrastructures can be removed, leaving only the architecture behind to melt away and return to the ocean.

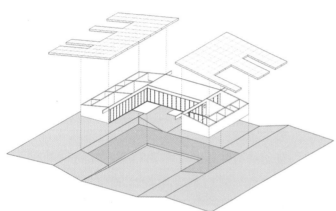

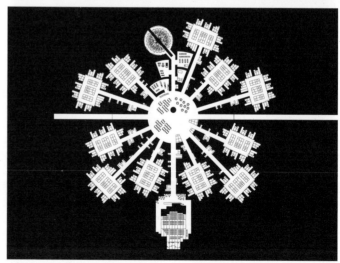

i/thee and Roundhouse Platform
Agg Hab, 2020
Clarendon, Texas, USA

Taken together, these self-supporting structures made from papier-mâché are over 6 m (20 ft) long and 2.4 m (8 ft) wide. The use of papier-mâché was born out of a budgetary limitation, a constraint that forced the team to think creatively and led to a new sustainable technology for casting shells using paper. 'Paper has many beneficial qualities over the alternatives,' notes Neal Lucas Hitch of i/thee. 'It is non-toxic, lightweight and relatively flexible. It is also possible to recycle paper back into itself – something that cannot be said of other recyclable materials – so its use becomes circular from an economic standpoint.'[6]

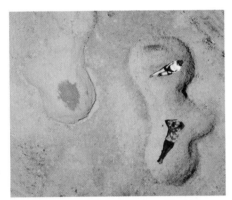

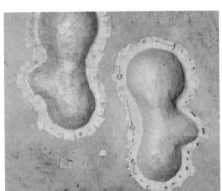

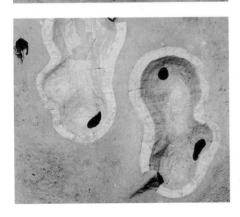

COLLABORATE

COLLABORATE
Together is better

Working together is easier than going it alone. A group effort can improve productivity and result in better outcomes for all involved, particularly when team members share a common goal but have different perspectives and areas of expertise. All of the homes in this chapter were built in collaboration with their end users. Architects brought their own skill sets into play as leaders, interpreters and mediators, and residents contributed their ideas, experiences and labour. The projects represent a shift from top-down solutions delivered by 'experts' in favour of participatory processes that synthesize multiple desires and points of view.

Chilean firm Elemental responded to urban overcrowding, low government subsidies and high property prices by developing a half-house model, with the long-term development of each home unfolding as a community effort (p. 60). Collaboration can also be used to open up a situation of constraint, as the team at Kofink Schels demonstrated with their renovation of the tiny TIA House in Almería, Spain (p. 63). The homeowner's inexperience instantly freed the project from convention: no meetings, just show-and-tell exchanges via smartphone that allowed the client to do most of the work himself.

Integrating residents into the creative process and long-term care of their homes is vital to the self-build social housing in Colombia by Ensamble AI (p. 61). In 2016, the National Federation of Coffee Growers built the first prototype for one of its workers in Sierra Nevada, updating the architects via WhatsApp. The following year, the design was developed through workshops with members of the Afro community of Sevilla, resulting in illustrated manuals that were handed out and will be open source, allowing more people to benefit. This idea is shared by students of the DesignBuildBLUFF programme at the University of Utah, who create, over the course of an academic year, a single-family home for a member of the Navajo Nation (p. 62). The students first learn about the indigenous architecture of the American Southwest in the classroom, before travelling to the remote desert town of Bluff to meet the residents, spending time with them to better understand their hopes and desires.

Elemental
Quinta Monroy, 2004
Iquique, Chile
Villa Verde, 2010
Constitución, Chile

Developers and governments typically address the need for low-income housing by drastically reducing square footage and situating homes on the periphery, a strategy that tends to cement the status quo, rather than helping to develop a thriving middle class. Moreover, it calculates and projects the needs of the end user by using mathematics alone, prioritizing cost analysis over desires or lifestyle. The team at Elemental pursue a different path, which aims to increase class mobility and stability. With their incremental housing model, they propose five basic design conditions that together comprise a viable solution: good location, harmonious growth over time, concern for social agreements between residents, no more than twenty-five families and delivery of a structure with 'middle-class DNA' that can be replicated. Placing themselves in the residents' shoes means, in practice, planning at the outset for the possibility of dignified expansion into a four-bedroom unit. It could also mean relocating a bathroom from the front door – where pipes are usually placed to cut costs – to near a bedroom and adding a bathtub. Ultimately, say the architects, it's a question of ensuring a balance between 'low-rise high density without overcrowding, with the possibility of upgrading from social housing to a middle-class dwelling'.[7]

Ensamble AI
Architectural System for Rural
Social Housing, 2012
Sierra Nevada de Santa
Marta, Colombia

This architectural system comprises five modular components – room, services, floor, eaves and ridge – which can be combined in numerous ways and finished with local materials. It is intended as a viable alternative to the randomly generated and serially built houses that are currently on the market. The individual components and assembly instruction are clearly detailed in the accompanying booklets, and the skills can be self-taught or learned in workshops.

'Our intention is for the project to reach different communities, where it can be adapted to need and replicated through self-construction by the residents, with adequate technical support,' note architects Juan Pablo Pardo and Simón Fique. 'In the long term, it has the potential to be a solution for the deficit of rural housing in Colombia, and be applied internationally owing to its low cost, efficient construction, and climatic, topographic and sociocultural adaptability. It is this application at an intermediate scale that can achieve the greatest impact.'[8]

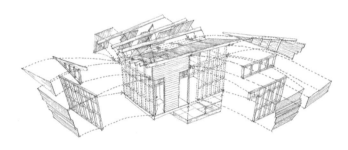

DesignBuildBLUFF
Silver Slice, 2019
Bluff, Utah, USA

The house was built by an all-female team of five students for a client who had spent many years without a permanent home, moving from one relative to the next. In a YouTube video documenting their progress, one of the team members says: 'We learned a lot about working with different cultures and people, and how important it is to take into account their perspectives.' Another notes: 'Our client really wanted to provide a home for her son. We just wanted to help her. Working together and compromising with the client is so important.'[9]

DesignBuildBLUFF
Badger Springs, 2015
Bluff, Utah, USA

The Navajo Nation occupies portions of northeastern Arizona, southeastern Utah and northwestern New Mexico. The town of Bluff is located near its northernmost chapters. Here, there are no hardware stores or lumber companies, so students and homeowners alike have to innovate on site with local and donated materials. Named after a nearby water source, this house was built for a client who assists victims of domestic violence. The design is intended to give a sense of protection and security to visitors in need of healing and recovery.

Kofink Schels
TIA House, 2016
Almería, Spain

Standing for 'This is Almería!', the name of the house signals the architects' radical acceptance of existing economic, bureaucratic and material limitations, and their willingness to search for solutions.

'The low budget forced us to think about new ways of planning,' they note. 'We realized that detailed plans didn't help the client to filter and communicate the important things, so we created a WhatsApp chat, which became a kind of digital sketchbook. He would send us photos of materials or unsolved problems, and we would reply with sketches and advice he could apply on site. We called the process "responsive design", as it was more of a reaction than a finalized planning.'

They add: 'The "role" of the architect has changed immensely. While architects are key figures in these processes, our role is usually far away from the visionary leadership envisioned throughout architectural history. Where architects want to play a role, they are often irrelevant, and where they refuse to play a role, they become vicarious agents. In this sense, the role might become more tragic than it is heroic, but this does not make it any less important.'[10]

DEMOCRATIZE

DEMOCRATIZE
Giving everyone a say

Whether built through an equitable design process or DIY self-build strategies, the homes in this chapter call for residents to take more control of how and where they live. The focus is on working together to nurture communities and improve access to safe, healthy homes, especially for those who reject or are rejected by the mainstream housing market.

Hustlenomics (p. 68) was informed by founder Nhlanhla Ndlovu's own experience of the substandard sheet-metal shacks in South Africa's townships. Aiming to provide better-quality homes for those on low incomes, it covers the build cost of four units per yard, which then share the rental income with the landowner. In Norway, Nøysom Arkitekter worked with a group of self-builders to design Svartlamon Experimental Housing (p. 68). Co-founder Haakon Haanes cites the 1970s self-build designs of Walter Segal in southeast London as a key influence. Their successor is nearby Church Grove (p. 73), a development of thirty-six energy-efficient homes.

Projects like these show how larger developments can be realized in the same democratic spirit by giving more control to the people who will live in them. In the 1990s, residents of the Granby Four Streets neighbourhood of Liverpool began a campaign to renovate the area after it was earmarked for demolition. They set up a Community Land Trust and worked with multidisciplinary firm Assemble to revitalize one of the terraces (p. 69). In 2015, it won the Turner Prize. The first social-housing scheme to win the Stirling Prize was Goldsmith Street in Norwich (p. 72), designed by architectural firm Mikhail Riches and former partner Cathy Hawley. It is also the largest development in the country to meet Passivhaus standards.

The POD Initiative, led by the Center for Public Interest Design in Portland, Oregon, is a coming together of architects and campaigners to develop transitional housing through collaborative design. After the city declared a housing emergency in 2015, hundreds of collaborators joined the project, leading to the Kenton Women's Village (p. 71), an inclusive and thoughtful approach to providing safe communities for people living on the streets.

Nhlanhla Ndlovu
Hustlenomics, 2015
Soweto, South Africa

Nhlanhla Ndlovu called his venture 'Hustlenomics' in reference to the people in his community who hustled to make ends meet, noting that there is no financing available for those without a steady job or payslips to prove it. Ndlovu replaced his own rickety shack with a brick-built house with the help of friends in a similar situation who had plumbing and carpentry skills. Working together meant they could buy materials in bulk to cut costs.

This newly formed team began helping with small-scale housing projects in Soweto, and Hustlenomics was born. The interlocking bricks are made from a mixture of clay, sand, cement and construction waste, some of which comes from sites where it was dumped illegally. They don't need to be fired in a kiln, and no construction skills are needed to lay them. After a cement foundation is laid, the bricks are dry-stacked to the height of the lintels above the doors and windows.

It takes about 9,000 bricks for each house, and using them enables the team to build a home in about a month. The bricks have generated much interest, with orders from 100 local stores and people in wealthier areas now wanting them. Ndlovu has since won several awards, including the Social Innovation Award 2018.

Nøysom Arkitekter
Svartlamon Experimental
Housing, 2017
Trondheim, Norway

The architects began developing the concept for the five self-build houses when they were still students, a process that took two years. The resulting homes rely on as few complex technological systems as possible. The loadbearing construction is a simple stud frame made from Norwegian spruce, and the foundations are concrete pillars, made on site by the self-builders, who also welded the reinforcing bars. Insulation made from hemp and wooden fibres line the walls. Wooden trusses spanning the roofs of each house allow for spacious, flexible double-height living areas below, while clerestory windows help provide natural ventilation. The glazed façades act, say the architects, as 'solar chimneys'.

A professional carpenter employed by the non-profit housing association, which leases the land from the City of Trondheim, provided assistance to the self-builders, who rent the houses long term. The project is unique in Norway, says the team, not only because of the area's special zoning designation as an urban ecological research area, but also because of the housing association's willingness to support initiatives that move into uncharted territory.

Assemble
Granby Four Streets, 2013
Liverpool, UK

The Granby neighbourhood of Liverpool, with a once-lively high street at the centre of the city's most racially and ethnically diverse community, was made nearly derelict by decades of poorly planned building initiatives. The demolition of all but four of its streets of Victorian terraces left the area sparsely populated and filled with boarded-up houses.

Over the course of two decades, a group of residents was fundamental to bringing these streets out of dereliction and back into use. In 2011, they started an innovative form of community land ownership with the intention of transforming the empty houses into affordable housing. Assemble, in collaboration with the Granby Four Streets Community Land Trust and Steinbeck Studios, designed a sustainable and incremental plan that builds on work already done by the community. The outcome of this vision has been the realization of a number of projects, including ten houses on Cairns Street, Granby Winter Garden and Granby Workshop, launched as part of the 2015 Turner Prize.

GIVING EVERYONE A SAY

Comunal
Social Production of Housing:
Exercises I and II, 2015 and 2016
Puebla, Mexico

After consultation with residents, architects Mariana Ordóñez Grajales and Jesica Amescua Carrera of Comunal identified two seemingly unrelated problems: a lack of housing appropriate to the climate and customs of the region, and an overabundance of bamboo.

Their original design (Exercise I) used the bamboo as a primary building material, consolidated key spaces and integrated low-cost technologies to collect, store and treat water. Cross-ventilation and hot-air exhaust chimneys were also added to maintain comfort throughout the year. Residents harvested the bamboo and built the houses using a modular technique to simplify and speed up the process.

Shortly after completion, however, Mexico's housing authority ceased its funding for self-built homes made from materials such as bamboo, wood and straw. Together with the local cooperatives, the architects designed a second model (Exercise II), which avoided using bamboo as a structural element.

Villagers could contribute labour to reduce the cost of their homes. Rainwater was harvested, and greywater reused. Basic bioclimatic strategies were implemented to combat the region's high temperatures. Spatially, the house responds to the customs and traditions of the Nahua people, who use the main hall as the location for the altar – the central element of the house – and for drying coffee and corn crops. Taking only a week to build, the revised system won an award from the housing authority and qualified for state funding.

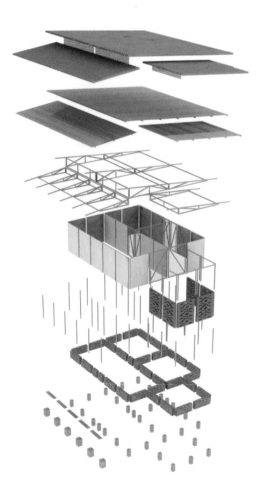

DEMOCRATIZE

Center for Public Interest Design
Kenton Women's Village, 2015
Portland, Oregon, USA

The results of a brainstorming session with nearly 100 architects, designers, activists and houseless people led to an agreed set of design parameters for a series of pods for houseless women: they had to be well insulated, transportable and cheap to make, as well as beautiful and dignified. Each person would have her own sleeping pod, and there would be a shared kitchen, dining space and bathrooms made from shipping containers. A key aspect of the design was that all elements had to be easily removed from site and transported to another location as needed. Architects from the POD Initiative reviewed the various designs and worked with residents to find the ones that worked best. The preferred option had angled walls and a small porch, which was applied to a series of fifteen pods for a veterans' residential village in Clackamas County, just outside Portland. Looking for ways to reduce costs and reuse materials, they worked with students from Portland State University, who designed a stage set for a music festival around the trusses needed for the framework. Once the festival was over, hundreds of trusses were ready to be made into pods.

GIVING EVERYONE A SAY

Mikhail Riches and Cathy Hawley
Goldsmith Street, 2019
Norwich, UK

This project reintroduces streets and houses to an area of Norwich otherwise dominated by modern blocks of flats. The design references a nearby sought-after area of Victorian terraced streets, known as the Golden and Silver Triangles. It is also low carbon, with all of the homes facing south. Once complete, it will be the largest social-housing scheme in the UK to achieve Passivhaus status, the highest certifiable standard of energy-efficiency.

The design provides two play areas and other landscape improvements to knit the scheme into the wider neighbourhood. Street widths have been kept narrow, only 14 m (46 ft). A reinterpretation of a traditional 'ginnel', or alleyway, runs through the centre of the scheme

to form a secure shared garden, encouraging a sense of community and providing a safe, visible place for children to play. The clients asked the designers to give residents their own front doors and access to open space, helping to promote a feeling of ownership and identity for each flat, reinforced by the different colours of the doors. Most houses are two storeys, with the occasional dormer to provide a third bedroom, and generous kitchen/dining rooms lie at the heart of each home.

The clients had some experience of Passivhaus standards in their smaller developments, and were keen to strive for this again to ensure the development had excellent environmental credentials. Their ambition was to achieve a relatively high-density but low-mass scheme, which recreates the look of the Victorian terraces before they were cleared after the Second World War.

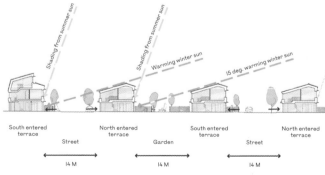

DEMOCRATIZE

Rural Urban Synthesis Society
Church Grove, 2021
London, UK

The community's vision here was to create socially, environmentally and economically sustainable neighbourhoods in the control of the residents, one that would provide a model other groups could replicate and offer an alternative to profit-led commercial developments. In addition to homes, the pilot project includes communal food-growing and gardening spaces, a shared laundry and publicly accessible playground. With a mix of property sizes and options to rent, buy or part-own, the aim of Church Grove is to reflect the social makeup of the local population, offering self-build opportunities for future residents who are given a discount based on the work they put in.

Carlo Ratti Associati
Livingboard, 2018
Karnataka, India

Italian design studio Carlo Ratti Associati teamed up with WeRise, a social enterprise based in Bangalore, to develop a prefabricated system that aims to improve housing in rural India. The Livingboard prototype gives communities the flexibility to build homes on top of a ready-made core that acts like a motherboard for the house, providing services like heat, water, electricity and waste-management, depending on the geography and infrastructure of the location. Once the core is in place, communities can then design and build their homes around it, choosing the functions they need, so that it becomes the heart of the home. A pilot version was developed for a site near Bangalore, where greywater will be recycled to irrigate farmland.

'The maker movement has shown how empowering it is to put the new fabrication tools in the hands of the people,' says Carlo Ratti, who is also director of the Senseable City Lab at MIT. 'An important challenge over the next few years will be to apply the same principle to construction – transferring the DIY attitude of Fab Labs to housing. This is the vision behind our design.'[11]

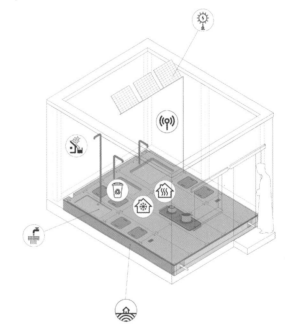

DIG

DIG
Thinking with your hands

When you pick up a shovel, you are thinking with your hands. Digging is an effective means of creating shelter, as many a camper can testify, and all of the homes included here have been built with earth or clay dug from the local area. Although a highly sustainable natural material with a long history of use, earth has been largely abandoned in favour of concrete. But homes built from it are durable and emit less CO_2 during construction. They also store passive energy, cutting down on fossil-fuel consumption.

For their design for a housing complex in Gando, Burkina Faso (p. 82), Kéré Architecture used earth for six adaptable modules arranged in a wide arc, reminiscent of the layout of a traditional Burkinaè compound. What is new is the use of thick adobe for the walls and earth bricks for the vaulted roofs, which were made by the community on site. Architect Marc Thorpe also intends to use bricks of red earth, formed and cured directly on site, as the primary building material for his Dakar Houses in Senegal (p. 83), which provide housing for employees of the Italian furniture brand Moroso.

In Accra, Ghana, Hive Earth devised a unique approach to rammed earth (p. 83). Ramming by hand, rather than pneumatically, they can influence the appearance of the walls by adding beads, shells and salts for decoration. The ancient technique of *pisé de terre* is also experiencing a resurgence in China, owing to the efforts of Professor Mu Jun of Beijing University of Civil Engineering and Architecture and the Bridge to China charitable foundation (p. 79), who note that soil can be used as building material for all climates.

In the US, where timber is abundant, building with rammed earth is not considered the norm. But architectural firm DUST chose it for a privately commissioned mountain retreat in southern Arizona (p. 85), precisely because the method approaches the landscape with respect. This belief is shared by Rama Estudio, in their design for Casa Lasso in Ecuador (p. 78). Because plantations of eucalyptus, imported from Australia in the late 1800s, have depleted the soil and inhibit the growth of native species, the design includes small islands of indigenous planting that will help regenerate the soil.

Rama Estudio
Casa Lasso, 2019
Lasso, Ecuador

This vacation home for a family and their guests in the province of Cotopaxi incorporates local materials and traditional methods to promote the education and practice of constructive vernacular systems. The region is near a volcano, and local wisdom leans towards earth materials that can absorb movement.

The roof is supported by five monolithic rammed-earth walls, or *tapia*, placed longitudinally along the site to protect the house from strong winds. Together, these form a blind façade that improves the home's thermal conditions. Interior walls employ bahareque (an indigenous method, similar to adobe, in which clay or mud is reinforced with sticks, cane or bamboo) to provide further stabilization. The house is solid, but also inviting.

**Professor Mu Jun and
Bridge to China
Building with Earth, ongoing
Macha, China**

Earth-building has a centuries-long history in rural China, ranging from adobe to pressed earth. In 2011, the Wu Zhi Qiao (Bridge to China) Charitable Foundation was set up to encourage volunteers to design and build footbridges and other facilities in remote areas, using green concepts. The Building with Earth programme is a collaboration with Beijing University of Civil Engineering and Architecture, among others.

Project leader Professor Mu Jun of Beijing University is helping to revamp this ancient wisdom with new technologies to help standardize the rammed-earth technique. The team initiated a model of learning by doing, with two master students and two craftspeople working alongside residents, who will then be able to build additional homes or become contractors to boost their income. A home built according to this model costs €65 to €100 per square metre, half the cost of a typical house. Rather than using soil, Mu used a mixture of clay, sand and gravel to improve water resistance, using a pneumatic hammer to achieve a firmer consistency. The homes are 5 degrees warmer in winter and 7 degrees cooler in summer, with 20 to 25 per cent of the embodied energy of a conventional residence.

THINKING WITH YOUR HANDS

Kéré Architecture
Gando Teachers' Housing, 2004
Gando, Burkina Faso

Architect Francis Kéré is a pioneer of sustainable building, as seen in this small complex of passive homes built from adobe and earth bricks. Although often considered a poor building material, earth produces a pleasant, self-regulating indoor temperature.

'No artificial ventilation or air-conditioning is necessary,' he says. 'This is the key advantage of these houses. They are cool during the heat for most of the year, but are also able to store warmth, which is crucial during the very short winter when temperatures can drop to around 15° C (59° F) at night.'[12]

In this way, the homes serve as an antidote to what Kéré calls the standard 'hot box' model, made from cement walls and a corrugated metal roof. He also discovered an important by-product of building with a local resource: a renewed sense of heritage.

'There is a socio-cultural element,' he explains, 'as people are more invested in buildings that incorporate a sense of comfort, and not just function. It is my belief that visionary architecture creates visionary inhabitants. It is easier to imagine a different future when you are already inhabiting one.'

Marc Thorpe Design
Dakar Houses, ongoing
Dakar, Senegal

Architect and industrial designer Marc Thorpe is currently at the concept level for a small community of live/work homes in Senegal. Each unit will comprise two apartments and one centralized workshop for welding or weaving, and eventually house employees of the Italian furniture brand Moroso, whose 'M'Afrique' line is handmade by local craftspeople.

Thorpe's work often focuses on reduction, so for inspiration he looked no further than the region itself. His idea is to build the new homes entirely from the red-earth bricks common to the area, which have isothermal properties that help to balance temperature. Since they can be sourced locally, reliance on imported materials is greatly reduced, contributing to cost savings and lower emissions during construction.

'Architecture is about people,' Thorpe says. 'The spaces we create should aim to lift the human spirit.'[13] Here in West Africa, he hopes to build a 'small village' that will support the everyday demands of its residents, where they can live without the need to travel for work, reducing their carbon footprint and maximizing family time.

Hive Earth
Rammed-Earth Housing, ongoing
Accra, Ghana

Rammed earth is not a new technique, but the way that Kwame Deheer and Joelle Eyeson of Hive Earth make use of it is. Their project was born from the desire to find a non-Western way of developing affordable housing. Although neither has formal architectural training, Deheer and Eyeson mastered the technique by experimenting with different soil combinations, such as mud and granite chippings, and producing hundreds of walls. These lessons have flowed into an eco-friendly demonstration home with solar energy and passive cooling, which is still under construction. The name of their company also has a personal note: the couple have a large beehive at home, and Eyeson sees parallels between making rammed earth and the labour-intensive workings that go on inside a hive.

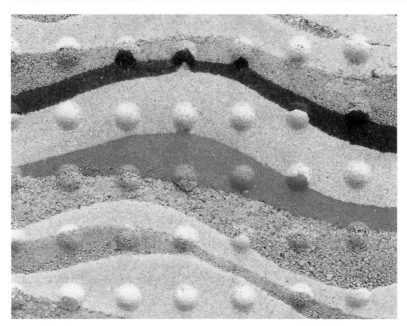

DIG

DUST
Tucson Mountain Retreat, 2012
Tucson, Arizona, USA

Located in the Saguaro National Park, this mountain residence for a couple exists harmoniously within its unspoiled landscape. It was designed by the multidisciplinary design studio DUST, an alliance of architects, craftspeople, artists, designers and builders with practices rooted in the master/builder tradition, and serves as a particularly beautiful demonstration of the aesthetic applications of rammed earth on a large scale. The walls have a natural striated beauty and warmth that echoes the cacti and changing light conditions of the surrounding desert. The inclusion of a music studio also allows the couple to integrate live music into their daily lives.

'We tend to look to the past for references, rather than to new product innovation,' says architect Cade Hayes. 'What can we learn from indigenous local builders, and those that came afterwards? We try to design all of our projects from this vantage point, common-sense design strategies that are rooted in place. This comes about with material selection, siting, orientation and harnessing all the free energy, heating and cooling we can.'[14]

EMPATHIZE

EMPATHIZE
A destiny of compassionate support

To empathize is to be sensitive to the needs of others, to take into account their view of the world and to think, feel and sense it from their perspective. The inclusive strategies in this chapter respond to the contemporary needs of a more diverse global demographic in an attempt to create more autonomy, spatial identity and equity.

We're all living longer, and it is estimated that by 2050 one in six of us will be over the age of sixty-five. This is reason enough to empathize with age-related health issues, which alter the visual perception of those affected and their experience of space. When architect David Burgher came across a mobile app to help the partially sighted person navigate the everyday, he immediately set to work on a device of his own. His Virtual Reality Empathy Platform (p. 93) is a tool for architects and other professionals to design better spaces for those living with dementia. Tomoaki Uno also believes that architecture can assist in personal and social care and healing, and designed Ogimachi House (p. 90) in Nagoya, Japan, specifically as a space of healing for the invalid mother of a young client.

This attention to special needs is shared by Jonathan Tate, founder of architectural firm OJT, who addressed the requirements of veterans in his Bastion housing complex in New Orleans (p. 91), and by the non-profit charity Social Bite, which supports the homeless and those with complex needs in Scotland. Their Social Bite Village (p. 93) comprises a staff-supported community of ten NestHouses, shared by two residents each.

The question of what constitutes a family nowadays is behind Beta's Three-Generation House (p. 94) in Amsterdam, a mini-apartment building for two households, which both gives everyone room to grow and anticipates changing dependencies. In Australia, Austin Maynard Architects' multigenerational Charles House (p. 96) is a flexible home for a family of five plus grandparents, providing a collection of spaces that can be opened up or closed off according to changes in age and use. After all, kids and grandparents are people, too.

Tomoaki Uno Architects
Ogimachi House, 2019
Nagoya, Japan

Commissioned by a son for his invalid mother, this home was designed with healing and safety in mind. Architect Tomoaki Uno chose to build it entirely from cedar and cypress, natural materials that have a simple beauty. They were joined together using the traditional *itakura* method, with boards slotted into posts without the need for nails. The living spaces are arranged within a central rectangular grid, surrounded by a two-storey corridor. On the ground floor is an open-plan living room, kitchen with dining area, toilet and bathroom, with four private rooms upstairs. To minimize disruptive external sights and sounds there are no windows, but rather a series of skylights in the roof – five fixed, the rest moveable – which provide natural light, as well as views of the sky. The overall result is one of quiet, contemplative serenity – and the client reports that his mother is enjoying life in her new home.

Office of Jonathan Tate
Bastion, 2018
New Orleans, Louisiana, USA

This housing complex for veterans in the Gentilly neighbourhood of New Orleans comprises 100 apartments, two per building, each with one to three bedrooms. The masterplan adheres to the 'core components of intentional neighbouring', as set out by the Generations of Hope Community Model, which emphasizes the forming and sustaining of caring relationships and treatment of vulnerable residents as friends, neighbours and family.

'In our context, it means that you're creating a community of neighbours in the traditional sense, who take a shared interest in assisting with and being a part of each other's lives to help facilitate re-entry into the non-military world,' notes architect Jonathan Tate. 'Our role, as with most projects, was to be excellent listeners for all those involved and interpret their wants and needs in creative ways. We receive a fair amount of comments from people that live there now. I'd say on a whole they all express a sense of dignity about their community.'[15]

Phased development

Building footprints

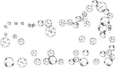
Preserved trees on site

Communal open space

Community programme

Unit clusters

SAWA Architecture
A House for a Victim, 2015
Ntarama, Rwanda

The process of building a home can itself be an empathetic experience to help ease trauma. That is part of the philosophy of Rev. Philbert Kalisa, founder of the non-profit Reach organization in Rwanda. Having been educated in the UK and US, he returned home in 1995, one year after the genocide, and now leads unity groups of survivors and their former perpetrators. As part of the reconciliation process, offenders build houses for victims' families, with seventy built so far.

Edward Dale-Harris of SAWA Architecture guided the construction of one of these homes, spending eight weeks on site with a group of newly released prisoners and some of the victims' families. It was important that the design echo the local vernacular, rather than be an interpretation of Western standards. The team's role was to suggest structural improvements, including rainwater collection, lime-stabilized earth plaster and a roof that provided more shelter. House for a Victim is a positive step towards peace-building as the country continues to move forward.

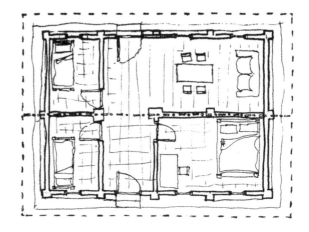

EMPATHIZE

David Burgher
Virtual Reality Empathy Platform
Galashiels, Scotland, UK

VREP is a new design application developed by architect David Burgher in partnership with the Dementia Centre, HammondCare, who specialize in dementia support, care and design. The disease interrupts the process of perceiving sensory information, and objects appear dimmer or less colourful than they are – a situation that can be frightening and confusing. The device allows architects, interior designers and healthcare professionals to see through the eyes of a fictional person with dementia, an immersive experience that can help them create more appropriate living spaces and help those living with the disease to lead more independent lives. Burgher anticipates that VREP can be used to design care homes or hospitals, assess existing buildings and environments, and improve quality of life – as well as the possibility of being adapted for other disorders.

'The technology takes this insight to another level,' he says, 'giving building designers first-hand experience of how dementia affects vision, so that we can design spaces that are far better suited to people with the condition.'[16]

Social Bite
Social Bite Village, 2018
Edinburgh, Scotland, UK

Social Bite is a charity that offers support to those affected by homelessness in the form of free meals and employment. Following conversations with those who had spent time in temporary accommodation, the team realized that the B&B model was not adequate for helping people transition to an independent life.

Social Bite Village responds to that need by providing a highly supported community for twenty people, with ten prefabricated houses for residents, a house for staff and a large community hub for eating and socializing. The houses are well insulated and energy-efficient, with each having two bedrooms, a shared kitchen and living area, and a separate toilet with a shower. Residents typically live in the village for up to eighteen months, during which they join in the life of the community, learn new skills and even begin working.

'Our overall ambition is to create a full-circle solution to the issue of homelessness – from housing support to employment,' say the team. 'By doing so, we hope to improve the lives of some of Scotland's most vulnerable people – swapping a destiny of poverty and exclusion for one of compassionate support and inclusion.'[17]

Beta
Three-Generation House, 2018
Amsterdam, Netherlands

In this model of multigenerational cohabitation, two households share a mini-apartment building, with grandparents at the top, and parents and children below. The upper unit has a lift and wide doors for a wheelchair, while the lower one has an office and garden. The two units are separate but accessed by the same entrance, with the possibility of being joined in the future.

'The position of the old double-helix staircase makes it possible to stretch the multigenerational living concept further,' says architect Auguste van Oppen. 'Two studio apartments could be added on the north façade to allow children to live at home when they get older.'[18]

By responding to needs across the generations, the design has made it possible for everyone to enjoy the benefits of living in an urban area, with access to work and cultural activities for all.

**Austin Maynard Architects
Charles House, 2017
Melbourne, Victoria, Australia**

In this multigenerational home in Melbourne, young and old have room to age and change. The clients – a family of five, plus grandparents – wanted a practical, low-maintenance house they could live in for at least twenty-five years and would adapt to their changing needs. The architects note that while they approve of increasing the number of people in a home, they also approve of a broader support network from each member of the family, welcoming a more complex understanding of what family life means and recognizing modern urban isolation, longer working hours, child-care issues, increases in retirement costs and inaccessibility to quality affordable housing – not only for the young, but also for the elderly.

Inside, the ground floor has a large kitchen and living area, and a study that can be incorporated into a separate living space and bath for the grandparents in the future. Upstairs, the parents have their own suite, reached by a bridge. The rest of the upper floor has sliding walls that allow for numerous configurations as the children get older.

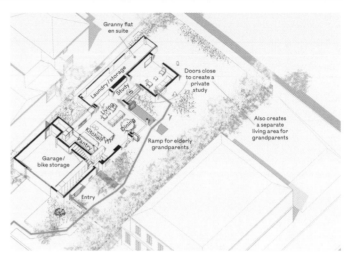

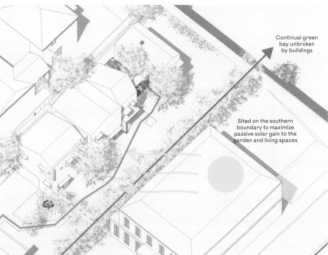

EMPATHIZE

Nishizawa Architects
House in Chau Doc, 2017
Chau Doc, Vietnam

For this co-living house in southern Vietnam, the architects created a calming respite for three families and their children within an open timber framework and plenty of interior planting. The open-to-the-outdoors residence is a continuous space that can be arranged into more intimate areas using moveable metal partitions. Chau Doc is situated on a branch of the Mekong River, a flood-prone area near the border of Cambodia. The prevailing residential typologies include floating homes and elevated timber-framed structures resting on concrete stilts

and wrapped in corrugated metal. These tend to be modest in scale, and often have lowered ceilings in accordance with the custom of sitting on the floor. The existing models inspired the team to adopt local customs, standards, materials and techniques in the construction of a home that is cost-effective and fits into its surroundings, but is larger and more flexible. To achieve this, they used a butterfly roof to open up the interior space and added rotating windows between the roof and façade to better regulate natural light and air circulation. The house is an antidote to the encroaching five-storey housing blocks that are making their way into the countryside – including on the plot next door.

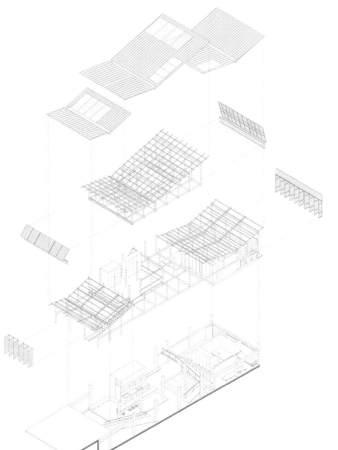

Husos Arquitecturas
A Guy, a Bulldog, a Vegetable Garden and the Home They Share, 2018
Madrid, Spain

In this apartment conversion, the architects paid close attention to the client's personal 'micro-realities' – in this case, those of a non-hetero doctor (and his pet bulldog) with irregular work/sleep patterns and a sensitivity to heat. They responded with 'socio-bioclimatic actions', which repurpose the existing floorplan to better reflect the needs of the two very different residents. The apartment is in a modern version of the traditional *corrala*, a block of flats with access corridors facing a shared courtyard. It was originally divided into small spaces along an east–west axis, which prevented cross-ventilation and resulted in extremely warm temperatures. Walls were removed to form an open living room, which keeps the space light but cool. It is dominated by a long wall of shallow shelves and a generous sleeping alcove with a sliding door. During the day, the alcove is used by the client for naps between shifts; at night, it serves as a guest bedroom or cinema room. Behind is a more private bedroom, with a dressing room and storage. Soft cotton knobs on the floor, held in place by suction cups, give Albóndiga the bulldog a place to rest and play. Instead of covering the walls with plaster, the architects used breathable mortar. The balcony overlooking the courtyard was transformed into a vegetable garden, with greywater from the shower used to irrigate the plants. This also helps keep the inside of the apartment cool without the need for air-conditioning.

SsD Architecture
Songpa Micro-Housing, 2017
Seoul, South Korea

With a model of 'connecting' that allows for endless increases and decreases in unit size, this variant on multigenerational housing in Seoul offers everyone who wants to live in the vibrant inner city the chance to live together longer in an affordable, flexible way. The complex comprises fourteen self-contained units within a unifying metal framework. What might be considered circulation space in other buildings is here the physical extension of individual units into a more communal domain. Not only do the interiors unfold according to different uses, they can also be recombined in any number of ways to accommodate shifts in life and work. The design also incorporates what the architects refer to as 'tapioca space', which extends perceptual boundaries and makes the architecture feel bigger, including bridges, balconies, corridors, voids and window views. Spatial requirements in South Korea are in constant flux owing to fluctuation in family size, resulting in ever-changing neighbourhoods as people move on to the next living space. The idea of diversity is evident even in the basement, which houses a café doubling as an auditorium and accessed by a stairway that also serves as seating – a kind of urban living room for everyone.

EMPATHIZE

Walllasia
Women's Dormitory and Meditation Building, 2018
Chonburi Province, Thailand

Women have often been overlooked in grand architectural projects. This serene dormitory and meditation building by Bangkok-based firm Walllasia seeks to redress the balance. Run by the Buddhist temple Wat Pa Watchira Banpot, the four-storey building contains 100 individual rooms with balconies, and a ground-floor multipurpose open space. It serves as the second home for female Dharma practitioners, who come here to meditate and reflect. Having already constructed a building at the complex ten years previously, Walllasia focused on the experience of former guests when designing the new space. Their feedback showed that security, peace and proximity to nature were vital concerns. Director Suriya Umpansiriratana notes it was 'the existence of things' that influenced the design, reflected in the large boulders at the centre of the structure that were simply left where they were and built around.[19] The large manmade pond at the front serves as a reservoir for water flowing down from the nearby hills. The soil excavated for the pond was then used to build the foundations of the dormitory.

FEEL

FEEL
The need for touch

Our homes provide us with mental and spiritual sustenance, and are the places where we feel safest, free to live out our dreams and express our authentic selves. This section looks at the sensory experience of home – its sights, sounds, scents, textures – and the emotional effects these have on us. These spaces tell personal stories and foster psychological wellbeing, but also reflect the modern balancing act between immersive digital technologies and our fundamental need for the physical world and human touch.

Artist and architect Phillip K. Smith III's Lucid Stead (p. 106), a converted and backlit homesteader's shack in Joshua Tree, California, offers just such a poetic experience of the place we call home. In Seattle, Abbey Dougherty, better known as Neon Saltwater, is also interested in how interior architecture affects people's moods. Her playfully dreamy Virtual Rooms (p. 108), with their luscious colours and sleek surfaces, are as energizing as they are wistful and personal. Ukrainian architect and designer Victoria Yakusha also posits the home and its contents as the location of identity. The hand-sculpted pieces in her Faina furniture collection (p. 107) have a soothing quality that is primal and familiar, and invites touch.

What if our homes could sense our emotional state? Philip Beesley's responsive and immersive environments, including Futurium Noosphere (p. 106), not only send out their own signals, but also respond to those given out by humans. Technology might even dissolve our preconceptions of the domestic altogether by enabling us to merge our own domestic spaces with those of others. Space Popular's Venn Room (p. 110) shows what can happen when real-world environments overlap, integrate or interface in virtual reality. Yet even as the digital age opens up new ways of connecting virtually, it's important to avoid what artist Lucy McRae describes as a 'touch crisis'. Compression Carpet (p. 113) reconnects users to their physical selves and helps to reduce isolation and loneliness. Perhaps one day it will also be used to treat illnesses or help train proprioception – our sixth sense – as we begin to make longer forays into space and think about inhabiting planets other than our own.

Phillip K. Smith III
Lucid Stead, 2013
Joshua Tree, California, USA

Light and colour can have a positive influence on our emotional wellbeing. Informed by minimalist art of the 1960s, artist and architect Phillip K. Smith III uses light to create large-scale site-specific sculptures and art installations. Lucid Stead is a modified homesteader's shack dating from the early 1900s and located on a desert property he bought several years ago in Joshua Tree, California. Rather than remove or renovate the tiny building, Smith transformed it into a luminous metaphor of home with only the slightest modifications. Every other row of siding was replaced with mirrors, which were also inserted into the door and window frames. By day, these mirrors function a bit like projection screens, reflecting the continuously shifting colours and movements of the sky. The house appears to lose all of its architectural contours and merge with the landscape. At dusk, these same mirrors emit coloured lights, powered by a remote solar array, which slowly change in hue and intensity. As the sky darkens, the building melts away, leaving only a silhouette of itself visible in thin lines and squares of light – a transformative version of home that lifts the spirits and can only be fully experienced by simply being there over time.

Philip Beesley Studio
Futurium Noosphere, 2019
Berlin, Germany

Our homes are formative places that can help us comprehend the larger world. When we feel at home, we explore things from a position of wonder and curiosity. This happy, non-judgmental interaction with our surroundings is a quality that Philip Beesley encourages. His work incorporates advanced digital visualization, industrial design, digital prototyping, electronics and mechanical engineering, and approaches architecture as a system of information that is shaped and formed much like living things are. His installation Futurium Noosphere demonstrates how a 'living architecture' might one day interact with its inhabitants, combining interactive light and sound with AI in the form of microprocessors arranged in mesh-like networks and protocells in small glass flasks, themselves miniature metabolizing worlds. The AI functions much like the neurology of the human brain and central nervous system, as the microprocessors communicate with one another and pass signals back and forth like synapses. The system observes, tracks and ultimately learns from its human visitors, and responds with its own tentative gestures. Lights turn on, fronds rustle and sounds emit as visitors move into its space.

FEEL

Yakusha Design
Faina, 2021
Kiev, Ukraine

The chairs, tables, nightstands, consoles and lamps in the Faina collection by Ukrainian designer Victoria Yakusha are all made from recycled metal frames covered in a natural material she calls *ztista*. Ukrainian for 'made from dough', it is a mix of clay, recycled paper, linen fibres, wood chips and straw, held in place with a cornstarch-based biopolymer. The material is eco-friendly and takes about five years to decompose. In developing the collection, Yakusha collaborated with local artisans who still use a modelling technique called *valkuvannia*, a rolling process used to cover solid surfaces with a mixture of straw, hay and natural clay, formerly used in the construction of Ukraine's traditional huts. The Faina collection is made by hand in limited editions, and its individual pieces are highly tactile and expressive. The design is intuitive and thus somehow familiar, tapping into archetypal emotions, as well as feelings of harmony and balance.

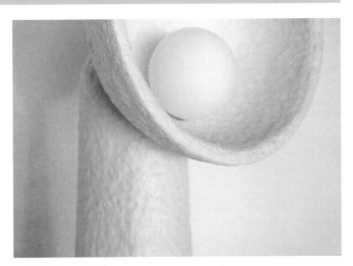

Neon Saltwater
Virtual Rooms, 2019–21
Seattle, Washington, USA

Interior designer and installation artist Abbey Dougherty, better known as Neon Saltwater, studied at the Cornish College of the Arts in Seattle, where she first learned how interior architecture can affect people's moods and experiences. Today, her clients include Barneys New York and Starbucks, but she is best known for the ambient and melancholy virtual rooms she posts on Instagram. With titles like 'Stripe Trip' (2021), 'Sharp Perfume' (2021), 'Sun Bars' (2019) and 'Eat Your Lip Gloss' (2020), Dougherty's interiors offer a sophisticated take on the LED-colour strip fad that has taken home decorating by storm. Colours can trigger or enhance any number of emotional states, and as we spend more time in mediated spaces, it is not surprising that we have also begun to fashion them to fit our dreams and desires – perhaps even more so than their real-life counterparts. Virtual interiors offer all sorts of possibilities for self-actualization precisely because they do not follow building codes or architectural norms. For Dougherty, they are places of fantasy and potential.

Pao Hui Kao
Paper Pleats, 2020
Eindhoven, Netherlands

Movement keeps us physically, mentally and emotionally alive, something we can lose sight of when spending long hours online or surrounding ourselves with too many industrially produced objects. Taiwanese designer Pao Hui Kao's Paper Pleats furniture collection – including stools, coffee tables, a dining table set, shelving, a space divider and a ceiling lamp – is made from flat sheets of tracing paper that are joined together with handmade rice water. The process encourages the paper to do what it does naturally when wet – wrinkle and shrink – and to express itself as a living, breathing material, one that can make a lasting impression. But Kao's experiments with paper are more than just material research.

'I was trained to fit into a system as a passive information recipient and a perfect follower of order,' she says. 'These slow, tiny movements from wet paper encouraged me to not be afraid of questioning the faith I believe in, against the huge framework around me.'[20]

The collection represents Kao's own search for authentic expression in a very personal journey.

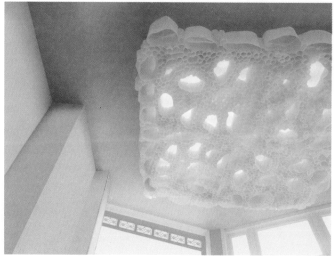

Space Popular
The Venn Room, 2019
Tallinn, Estonia

Lara Lesmes and Fredrik Hellberg of London-based Space Popular are the duo behind the Venn Room (these pages and p. 112), a mixed-reality environment in which physical and virtual worlds merge. The idea takes into account already existing 6DoF technology, which enables users to move about physically in virtual spaces, as well as triggering other senses. This opens up a multisensorial dimension to what is essentially an audio-visual experience. But as we move our bodies in these simulated worlds, we are also physically moving in the real world we inhabit, which has consequences for the layout of our physical home. Once we begin to invite others into our VR space, based on our real-life one, bits of their physical homes will begin to mingle with our own.

'In this new shared space, it might be necessary to move objects in your own home so you can sit at a virtual table with your guest,' note the designers. 'Or you might have certain furniture layouts for specific conversational partners. All of these things can then be merged with virtual objects or decorations that can be changed, reused or disposed of over time.'[21]

So who owns the furniture or kitchen utensils in these new merged spheres? 'Just as you may choose a nice bookshelf as a backdrop for a video call, sections of your home will become part of our fully embodied encounters with others in virtual reality,' they add, 'not only for self-expression, but also to prevent you from literally bumping into walls. And thus the global home is born, the result of many homes being brought together into one large, shared space to which every participant has necessarily contributed.'

THE NEED FOR TOUCH

Lucy McRae
Compression Carpet, 2019
Los Angeles, California, USA

Sci-fi artist and body architect Lucy McRae can imagine a future in which perfume takes the form of a pill ('Swallowable Parfum') or human bodies can be modified by mixing edible gene recipes in the kitchen ('Make Your Maker'). She believes that technology has the potential to disconnect us from one another. To stave off this 'crisis of touch', she developed the Future Survival Kit, which includes 'deeply immersive tools for the future, designed as antidotes to our submissive nature towards technology'.[22] Included in this kit is Compression Carpet, a low-tech machine for hugging, which looks like a giant sleeping bag or padded cocoon. It is operated by two people, one of whom is grasped in the machine's cushioned arm, while the other turns a crank to increase pressure. Not only does the design bring people into contact with one another – since the person being held must communicate with the one operating the machine – but it also decreases stress and soothes the senses, like the pressure of a real human embrace. Studies have shown that when people meet in a long, deep squeeze, the hormone oxytocin is produced, which helps us form positive bonds. Touch keeps us physically, mentally and emotionally alive. Most people, McRae notes, have a glazed look in their eyes after a three-minute embrace.

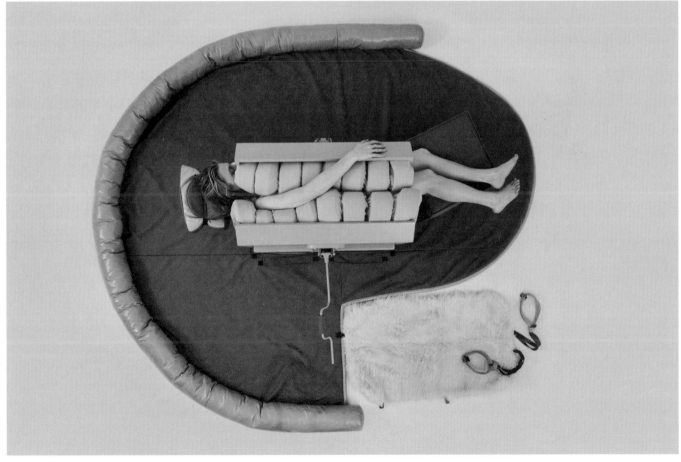

FILL

FILL
Soil is everywhere

Of all the strategies for building a safe, low-cost home, building with earth-filled bags or plastic bottles must be one of the simplest and most sustainable. Architects began experimenting with earthbags in the 1970s as a cost-effective way of building homes, and they are now used for emergency shelters and luxury holiday accommodation, and even proposed as habitats in space. Few construction materials can rival them in terms of affordability, strength and portability, but where they excel is in the simplicity of the construction technique.

Nader Khalili of CalEarth (pp. 118, 120) developed the SuperAdobe system in the 1970s, and later presented it at a NASA symposium that discussed ways to build on the Moon and Mars using onsite materials. Like many earthbag builders, CalEarth focuses on empowering individuals to build a safe home, and SuperAdobe buildings can now be found in over fifty countries. Yutaka Sho of GA Collaborative cited the straightforwardness of earthbag building as one of the reasons they chose the method for two prototype homes in Masoro, Rwanda (p. 121), the first of their kind in the country.

In neighbouring Uganda, David Monday and Johnmary Kavuma of Upcycle Africa swapped earthbags for plastic bottles, building their first plastic-bottle house in Mpigi, near Kampala, in 2014 (p. 123). Although people were sceptical to start with, within five years the team had built 110 homes, using over 1.6 million discarded plastic bottles. Similar homes have been built in Algeria, where engineer Tateh Lehbib made a home for his grandmother after flooding affected the Sahrawi Refugee Camp where he was born. Lehbib's idea caught the attention of the UN High Commissioner for Refugees Innovation Service, who supported the building of twenty-seven plastic bottle homes across each of the five refugee camps in Algeria (p. 122). Camp communities formed groups to gather and prepare the building materials, with one collecting the bottles, another filling them with sand, and another – a team of trained masons – building the homes. Wishing to share his knowledge, Lehbib plans to build a centre for sustainable construction to help more people build their own homes.

CalEarth
Eco-Dome and Earth One Vaulted House, 2003 and 2007
Hesperia, California, USA

Both Eco-Dome and Earth One Vaulted House were built using the SuperAdobe building technology, developed by CalEarth founder Nader Khalili, which uses sandbags filled with damp earth and arranged in layers as a primary building material. Strands of barbed wire placed between each layer act as both mortar and reinforcement, and stabilizers such as cement, lime or asphalt emulsion can be added.

Eco-Dome is an energy-efficient 'tiny home', which has been engineered to meet and surpass all structural building codes, including California's requirements for seismic destructive testing. Earth One Vaulted House is CalEarth's prototype three-bedroom SuperAdobe home. It features all the standard amenities (heating, air-conditioning, fireplace, kitchen), demonstrating the ability to integrate such technologies into the system. Both homes are modular designs: Eco-Dome is often built as a double-dome to provide additional bedrooms, and Earth One is available in multiple configurations.

CalEarth
Homey Dome, 2019
Taos, New Mexico, USA

Harry Schaeffer built Homey Dome after participating in a workshop at CalEarth. 'Earthbag construction is best suited to people who are willing to work hard, but don't have much money,' he says. 'The materials are cheap and can be found nearly anywhere in the world, but it takes some serious muscle to conjure a home from the earth beneath you. I do believe any able-bodied person can accomplish it given enough time, but it's not as easy as it looks. Housing is a human right, and we have more than enough resources to put a roof over everyone's head. Earthbag would be great for mainstream construction, it just lacks mainstream awareness.'[23]

Homey Dome took a total of 108 days to build, with filling and laying the earthbags taking around two months after digging the foundation and before applying the plaster. Harry lived on site throughout the build – first in a tent, before moving into the bedroom dome – working on the project nearly every day.

GA Collaborative
Masoro House, 2013
Masoro, Rwanda

The process of building a small three-bedroom home in Masoro, Rwanda, was a learning experience for all concerned. Built using earthbag construction, it is the first of a series of homes for members of the local women's cooperative.

'During one of the early workshops, we discovered that there are many single men in Rwanda in need of rental rooms,' says architect Yutaka Sho of GA Collaborative. 'Men cannot marry if they are not able to build a home for the family. Single women can be hired as live-in maids, but single men have a tougher time. Yet the government housing typology promotes the ideal of the nuclear family with bedrooms off the living room.'[24] This design makes each bedroom accessible from a covered corridor.

The architects realized that the technology worked better in arid areas and that the houses needed ongoing maintenance. The polypropylene sacks moved as they settled, the lintels had to be replaced, and the cement coating that protected the polypropylene from UV light disintegrated. The team returned two years later to remove the plaster, attach chicken wire, and then reapply the plaster on top, making the cost per house more expensive. The high cost was partly due to the fact that the sacks had to be imported, since Rwanda does not have a petrochemical industry that can produce them.

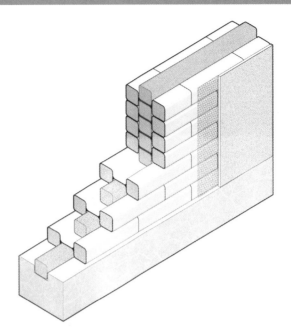

SOIL IS EVERYWHERE

121

Tateh Lehbib
Plastic Bottle Houses, 2017
Tindouf, Algeria

Twenty-seven of Tateh Lehbib's Plastic Bottle Houses were built at the Sahrawi Refugee Camp, with each requiring around 6,000 bottles, packed with sand and then stacked. Inside, the walls are covered in a layer of earth and straw, and finally with cement. Houses in the camps have usually been made from adobe, fabric and metal sheets, and often destroyed by sandstorms and torrential rains. Lehbib's circular designs allow the walls to hold together with more compression, and the bottles are bound together with cement or clay.

Albatoul Mohammed was given one of the houses after the family's home was damaged by floods in 2015. 'At first I refused it,' she says. 'But we desperately needed the house – our son has special needs and finds it very hard to live in these tough conditions. I'm very proud of the design, and that it was the idea of a refugee who saw first-hand how his people were suffering. We can sleep safely during sandstorms and heavy rain. There's no substitute for safety, because we can't live without it.' [25]

Upcycle Africa
Round Houses, 2015
Mpigi, Uganda

After losing family members to accidents caused by the sheer number of discarded plastic bottles in Uganda, David Monday and Johnmary Kavuma co-founded Upcycle Africa to build safer homes, clean up their local area and provide jobs for people in need. 'My aim is to let the world know the value of a bottle,' Monday says. 'If people had not thrown the bottles away, my brother would not have died.'[26]

It takes about 15,000 bottles to build each one of Upcycle Africa's houses. Interior walls are plastered, but the exterior is left unfinished to show what the homes are made from. Roofing materials include sheet metal, rubber from old car tyres, papyrus, spear grass and timber. Builders will often make patterns with the different colours, and an ice-cream company even funded a house in the shape of one of their vans.

ZAV Architects
Presence in Hormuz 2, 2020
Hormuz, Iran

For their colourful project located on Hormuz Island in the Persian Gulf, Tehran-based studio ZAV Architects employed CalEarth's SuperAdobe system of earthbag architecture, developed by Nader Khalili (see pp. 118–20). According to the team, the existing construction knowledge at a local level was basic, but by using the SuperAdobe method, residents participating in the project could learn and develop new skills. By modifying the original building technique, the architects were able to alter the shape of the tops of the two hundred or so domes that comprise the holiday village, making them both wider and lower to better reflect the surrounding landscape and skyline.

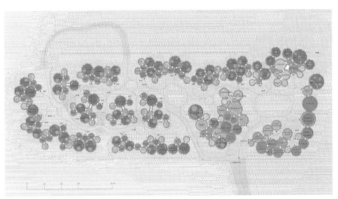

SOIL IS EVERYWHERE

123

SOIL IS EVERYWHERE

FLOAT

FLOAT
A different relationship

Building a big concrete wall is the typical response when trying to protect places from flooding, but for UK designer Matthew Butcher, this isn't always a good idea. New methods and a different relationship with the environment are needed. To facilitate this new relationship, Butcher created a series of projects in response to the unique landscape of the Thames Estuary – including Flood House (p. 130), Silt House (p. 131) and Bang Bang House (p. 131) – where 1.3 million people and £275 billion worth of property and infrastructure exist alongside increasing tidal flood risk.

Another innovative design for homes on the water is Schoonschip (p. 132), a floating, self-sufficient neighbourhood in Amsterdam, comprising forty-six homes built on thirty pontoons. Initiated by the people who would eventually live there, the project was planned by design studio Space&Matter with a string of collaborators, including architects who worked with each household to design their own homes. Bjarke Ingels Group also turned to the waterfront for Urban Rigger (p. 134) to provide student housing in Copenhagen's underused harbour. Nine shipping crates are stacked in a circle to create twelve floating studio apartments, centred around a winter garden. And in the US, artist Mary Mattingly explores our relationship with water and waste, and the differences between land and water-based regulation. For WetLand (p. 135), she transformed an old boat into a floating sculpture – part-houseboat, part-office, part-farm – which includes rainwater collection and purification, greywater filtration, dry composting, and vegetable, hydroponic and floating gardens.

An area that is given little attention in floating architecture is the underside of a boat, prompting Architectural Ecologies Lab to design the revolutionary Buoyant Ecologies Float Lab (p. 136), which works like an upside-down reef and has the potential to create new habitat for marine life, reduce coastal erosion, generate power and build floating communities. The team is also working on designs for floating communities in the Maldives (p. 136), where rising sea levels mean that land is disappearing rapidly, and everything from food to building materials and energy is shipped from somewhere else.

Matthew Butcher
Flood House, 2016
Thames Estuary, UK

Flood House started off as a temporary floating house-like structure as part of a public arts programme in the Thames Estuary. The project addresses new ways of living with the threat of flooding by embracing the movement of the tide. Its strange form references the fishing sheds, bunkers and wrecked boats littered across the landscape, and contrasts dramatically with the vastness of the mudflats. It acts as a premonition: if we cannot curb global warming, then the design becomes a potential model for future living in this landscape.

Made from plywood and weatherboard, the house floats on three steel pontoons. The weathervane by artist Ruth Ewan is titled *All Distinctions Levelled*, referring to the concept of social equality and to the rise and fall of the tides. Flood House was conceived in collaboration with the UCL Institute for Environmental Design and Engineering, and was funded through an award from the Bartlett Faculty of the Built Environment Materialisation Grant programme.

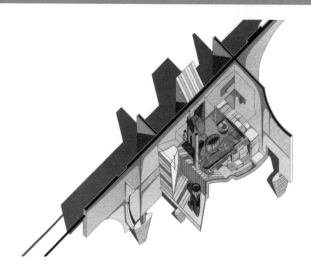

Matthew Butcher
Silt House, 2015
Thames Estuary, UK

Silt House is a series of imagined dwellings that explore the complex relationship we have with the threat of flooding. Designed for the marshlands on the south side of the Thames Estuary, the curved, shell-like building allows water to flow around and over it, and for mud to settle on top of it. At high tide, floodwater is used to flush the sewage system. In the winter, the house buries itself in the silt and sediment of the river for added protection against the cold. Architect Matthew Butcher describes Silt House as an example of 'lone architecture facilitating a frontier existence sited on the edge of a new flood wilderness'.[27]

Matthew Butcher
Bang Bang House, 2017
Thames Estuary, UK

This project is a conceptual house on the coast of Canvey Island in the Thames Estuary, moored within a metal enclosure. When the tide is up, the building floats on a series of pontoons; when the tide is out, it rests on the mud flats. Inside are a series of micro-dwellings that allow inhabitants the chance to escape harsh weather, as well as the sound of the building as it bangs around its 'cage' during high tide. The undulating floors of the various structures within the house encourage residents to move around as if carried along on a wave, or navigating across the bleak mud flats of the island.

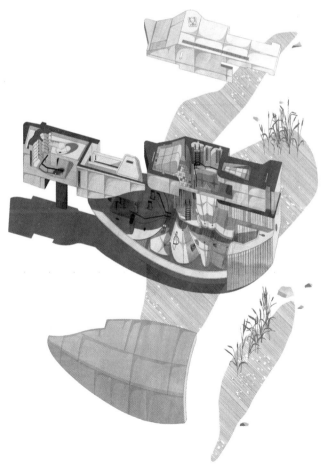

Space&Matter
Schoonschip, 2021
Amsterdam, Netherlands

On a small scale, Schoonschip proposes inventive solutions to some of the challenges that come with global climate change. 'Schoonschippers' apply simple yet effective innovations to bring environmental benefits, as well as social and economic ones.

Developing the project was a hugely complex operation that took years to realize. Like all of the projects in this chapter, Marjan de Blok, Thomas Sykora and the pioneers behind Schoonschip had to navigate a time-consuming array of laws and regulations to realize their dream. Occasionally this meant negotiating special permissions, because this type of collective development was the first of its kind in the Netherlands.

Most of the components – sustainable building practices, collective private commissioning, building a home on the water – are not new, but combining them in one project had not been done before. One way to reduce costs was for two households to share a floating plot, but the developers did not realize the legal complications this would entail. Floating semi-detached houses did not exist, and it was challenging to secure mortgages for two households sharing a moveable property. They now share their knowledge to help others create sustainable floating neighbourhoods.

Bjarke Ingels Group
Urban Rigger, 2016
Copenhagen, Denmark

This project uses the familiar form of shipping crates to create floating student housing in Copenhagen harbour. Student numbers are rising in Denmark, and Urban Rigger is a way to both accommodate them and make use of the city's underused docklands. The architects stacked nine containers in a circle to form twelve studio apartments around a central winter garden, which acts as a meeting place. Arranging the containers in a triangular shape helped to minimize the footprint of the floating pontoon, and the team also left gaps between each container to open up the courtyards and frame views between the floating homes. Using shipping crates provides a framework for a flexible building type that can be replicated in other waterfront cities, where housing is needed but space is limited.

FLOAT

Mary Mattingly
WetLand, 2017
Philadelphia, Pennsylvania, USA

Resembling a partially submerged building, WetLand is a floating sculpture that integrates nature with the built environment. It first appeared at the Philadelphia Fringe Festival in 2014, and eventually found a home at Bartram's Garden in Philadelphia, in partnership with the University of Pennsylvania's Penn Program in Environmental Humanities. WetLand was built entirely from the urban waste stream, with space inside to live, work, perform and grow food. Outside are vegetable gardens and systems for collecting, purifying, and storing water.

'After a design phase, I looked for a used vessel that would fit the budget, was large enough to house a performance space and residency, and could accommodate the visual perception I was trying to achieve,' says artist Mary Mattingly. 'At its heart, WetLand is a call to action. It asks people to reconsider living systems and interdependencies, and to pave pathways to create more public commons in largely privatized cities.'[28]

Buoyant Ecologies Float Lab
Architectural Ecologies Lab, 2019
Oakland, California, USA

This cutting-edge prototype for an ecologically productive floating breakwater merges expertise from design, advanced digital manufacturing and marine ecology to imagine a new kind of architecture for climate adaptation. It is made from fibre-reinforced polymer using a reusable mould, and is also modular, allowing multiple prototypes to be arranged together in a chain. The two mounds comprising the 'roof' are covered in textured bumps and ridges, designed to channel water into small ponds, and echoed by the shape of the hull below, whose contoured peaks and troughs provide habitat for various invertebrates. Chandelier-like columns hanging from the hull encourage more invertebrate settlements. Water flowing past this underwater landscape brings plankton and other nutrients, helping to promote ecological diversity. In large masses, this type of biological growth can help attenuate wave action and reduce coastal erosion, one of the primary impacts of climate change and sea level rise. The entire underside of the prototype was covered with creatures within a few months of its launch in San Francisco Bay in 2019.

Waterline
Architectural Ecologies Lab, 2020
Dhangethi, Maldives

Architectural Ecologies Lab scaled up the ideas formulated with the Buoyant Ecologies Float Lab (left) to create a floating community in the Maldives. Focusing on the island of Dhangethi, the team looked at the technologies and skills available and developed different proposals for modular floating communities. Local students critiqued the work and raised questions concerning issues such as storms and excessive rain.

Developed by students Emma Lou and Cera Ceo, Waterline shows how the island's traditional crafts could be transferred to floating communities. Above the fibreglass hull, bamboo is used as the structural framework, with palm-frond thatching providing shelter. The designers proposed replacing the island's existing concrete harbour with a mangrove one and floating marketplace, forming a spine through the island with a mangrove nursery and floating homes on the opposite side.

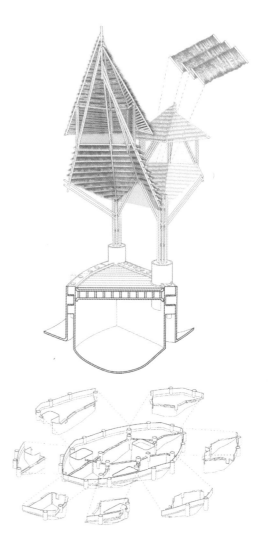

A DIFFERENT RELATIONSHIP

GROW

GROW
We are all biodegradable

In the hunt for healthier, more sustainable options in building homes, architects and builders are rediscovering plant-based materials such as timber, cork, straw and hemp, and fusing them with new technology. Rich in feeling and character, natural materials have a special resonance and bring buildings to life. As the homes included here demonstrate, plant-based materials can also simplify how buildings are made, meaning they can be dismantled and reused, or even returned to the earth at the end of their life.

It was thinking about what happens during the life cycle of a building that resulted in Cork House (p. 142), a radical yet simple response to the complexities of mainstream housebuilding. Like cork, hemp is another natural material experiencing a comeback. London studio Practice Architecture used hempcrete extensively for a low-carbon house on a hemp farm in Cambridgeshire (p. 143). Tav Group, based in Haifa, Israel, also used hempcrete for clients who wanted their home to be an archetype of sustainable building that would blend with its surroundings (p. 147).

Two homes in this chapter use low-grade timber that might otherwise be discarded: House for Marebito (p. 145), a small guesthouse in the mountains near Nanto, Japan, and Hannah Design Office's Ashen Cabin (p. 146) in Upstate New York. In Brazil, the façade of Zunino House (p. 147) by Estudio Campana was inspired by the indigenous *oca* houses, and coated in shaggy palm-tree fibres.

In the future, we might be able to not only grow materials to build with, but also whole buildings that can repair themselves. The non-profit research group Terreform ONE is part of a growing movement that is taking grown or biomaterials to the next level. With Fab Tree Hab (p. 150), they propose using the ancient technique of pleaching, grafting trees together to form a single, living system. The team at NASA Institute for Advanced Concepts, together with Redhouse Studio, are exploring technologies that could grow habitats on the Moon and Mars and beyond from mycelium, envisioning a future where human explorers can bring a compact habitat into space that will survive the journey – and thrive (p. 153).

**Matthew Barnett Howland
Cork House, 2019
Berkshire, UK**

Cork House comprises a radically simple method of plant-based construction, with a highly innovative self-build kit-of-parts designed for disassembly. Granules of low-grade cork are cooked and bound together in their own resin to form the building blocks, which are milled into individual, interlocking shapes that can be assembled on site without the need for glue or mortar. As well as the structure, cork blocks are used for insulation and the finish, inside and out. At the end of the house's life, the cork blocks can be dismantled, shredded and crumbled into soil, to start the cycle all over again.

'Cork House embodies a strong whole-life approach to sustainability,' says architect Matthew Barnett Howland. 'The system is dry-jointed, so that all 1,268 cork blocks can be reused, recycled or returned to the biosphere. The resulting form is a progressive reimagining of the simple principles of ancient stone structures, such as Celtic beehive houses. Internally, the exposed cork creates an evocative sensory environment – walls are gentle to the touch and even smell good, the acoustics are soft and calm, and copper pipes gleam in the shadows of the corbelled roof pyramids.'[29]

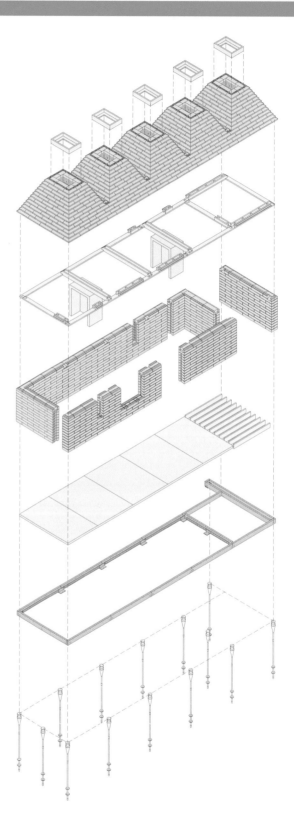

Practice Architecture
Flat House, 2019
Cambridgeshire, UK

Flat House demonstrates how a low-tech approach and bio-based materials can be combined with offsite construction to create a scalable, low-impact and beautiful building. The design draws from centuries-old material technologies and construction principles, re-rationalizing them for contemporary building techniques. The client, Margent Farm, develops hemp-based products, and created a new corrugated sheet cladding made from hemp fibre and a sugar-based resin derived from agricultural waste such as corn cobs. Hempcrete has two drawbacks, however: its lack of loadbearing strength and the time it takes to dry. To solve these problems and speed up construction, the architects worked closely with engineers and materials specialists to develop prefabricated timber-framed panels infilled with hempcrete from plants grown on the farm. These structural panels arrived on site ready to use, and were raised into place in only two days. Inside, they were left exposed to reveal the organic nature of the construction.

WE ARE ALL BIODEGRADABLE

Practice Architecture
Polyvalent Studio, 2019
Cambridgeshire, UK

Polyvalent Studio is a radically low-carbon, flexible space that can be built anywhere. Built at the same farm as Flat House (p. 143), the project was conceived within the parameters of the 1968 Caravan Act and did not require planning permission. The design is a prototype for a scalable studio that can be adapted with minimal modification to multiple sites.

Imagined in section, the form drew inspiration from cantilevered barns normally used for storage. The minimal palette of materials comprises hempcrete, a spruce stud and plywood superstructure, wood-fibre insulation and the hemp-fibre bioresin corrugated cladding sheets developed by Margent Farm. Designed by students from Unit 7 at London Metropolitan University, led by David Grandorge and Paloma Gormley, and built in just twelve days, the project is an exemplar of low-embodied energy design.

VUILD
House for Marebito, 2019
Nanto, Japan

The design of House for Marebito, located in the tiny village of Toga, near the city of Nanto, is based on the area's steep-roofed homes, designed to withstand heavy snowfall. With only six hundred residents, over half of whom are aged sixty-five or older, the village is in danger of disappearing. The architects wanted to build a house for guests when visiting relatives in the village, and to create jobs. They proposed a networking system, which allows the construction process from material procurement to installation to be completed within a 10-km (6-mile) radius of the site. A cheap but high-performance digital-fabrication machine was installed at a local lumber mill, and was used to slice logs that did not meet the standards for wider distribution into wooden boards suitable for machining. It was vital to keep the wooden parts of the building small and easy to transport. The house was designed like a piece of flat-pack furniture, so that it can be assembled with simple tools and without the need for scaffolding.

WE ARE ALL BIODEGRADABLE

Hannah Design Office
Ashen Cabin, 2019
Ithaca, New York, USA

For this cabin in Upstate New York, the architects upcycled beetle-infested ash trees into an abundantly available and sustainable building material. Irregular logs were sawn into naturally curved boards of varying thicknesses, using an industrial robotic arm with a custom bandsaw attachment. The boards were then arranged into interlocking SIPs (structural insulated panels), with offcuts integrated into the assembly to reduce waste. The team used 3D-printed concrete for the support structure, floor, fireplace and fitted furniture. The façade assembly was fully ventilated and detailed to manage shrinkage and transformation of the wooden boards to offset the air-drying process, and does not require an additional rainscreen.

The cabin sits on the edge of a field along a ridge, overlooking the landscape. Over time, the exterior will weather and grey naturally, creating a more nuanced distinction between the two predominant material systems: concrete and wood.

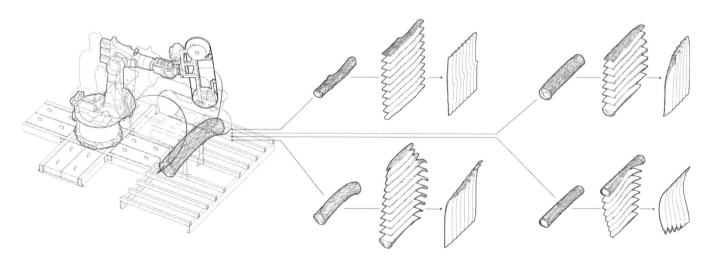

Estudio Campana
Zunino House, 2016
São Paulo, Brazil

Inspired by Brazil's indigenous *oca* houses, the front façade of this luxury home is coated in shaggy fibres from the piaçava palm plant.

'Piaçava grows in abundance in the northeastern part of Brazil, and is an important part of the indigenous vernacular culture,' note the designers. 'The so-called *oca* house is a giant oval structure covered with this plant, housing several families within a tribe. Piaçava is widely used as a roofing material, as well as for household items such as brooms and baskets. Our design for Zunino House represents the combination of values we believe are pillars to a better future and are linked to one theme: preservation. The architecture integrates the structure with the environment, creating a different relationship between people and nature. It doesn't pollute or create waste, because it uses sustainable or repurposed materials. The house is located on a noisy street and is fully exposed to the sun, so we knew that piaçava would be the perfect building material.' [30]

Tav Group
Ein Hod Ecological House, 2016
Ein Hod, Israel

From conception to completion, this private home located within an artists' village on the southern slopes of Mount Carmel, facing the Mediterranean Sea, was designed and constructed with the environment in mind. The lower section is made from stone excavated from the site, and the upper section is made from hemp hurds, bound with hydraulic lime and cast in a timber frame. This construction method, along with the use of rammed-earth partitions inside the house, provide excellent insulation and thermal mass. Outside, walls are coated with lime-based natural plaster; inside, the surfaces have been treated with a thick layer of earth-based plaster. The house also features ecological infrastructure systems including greywater purifying and reuse, rainwater collection and channelling into an underground cistern, compost toilets, rooftop solar panels and passive air-conditioning. The all-natural finishes of sand and earthy tones echo the colour palette of the surrounding landscape.

Terreform ONE
Fab Tree Hab, 2012
Cambridge, Massachusetts, USA

The architects of Fab Tree Hab question the convoluted time- and energy-consuming process of growing trees for construction. Why go to the trouble of growing trees, cutting them down with power tools, burning fuel to transport them, using energy to saw them into pieces, shipping them, and then turning them into a building, only to demolish it and dump the waste in landfill? With this project, they propose eliminating all of that processing of natural materials, and instead using the ancient technique of pleaching to shape living trees into the form of a house.

'When the tree is big enough, a living structure is grafted into shape using prefabricated CNC reusable scaffolds,' the architects note. 'Home, in this sense, becomes indistinct and fits itself symbiotically into the surrounding ecosystem. It can become fully integrated into an ecological community. Traditional anthropocentric doctrines are overturned, and human life is subsumed within the terrestrial environs.' [31]

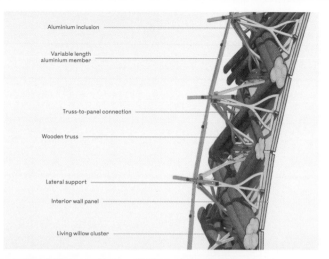

Aluminium inclusion
Variable length aluminium member
Truss-to-panel connection
Wooden truss
Lateral support
Interior wall panel
Living willow cluster

MAP Architects
Accretion Project
Kaafu Atoll, Maldives

This project looks at using accreted coral as a method for growing houses in the Maldives. Although the practice is now illegal, coral used to be sawn into bricks and used as a building material on the islands. Inspired by the work of Thomas J. Goreau, the team began with the steel-reinforced skeleton of a housing unit, which is then lowered into the sea. A low-voltage current is passed through the frame, and minerals from the seawater begin to bind to it through the process of electrolysis at an accelerated rate two to six times faster than naturally occurring coral growth. Layer upon layer of minerals build up over time to form a concrete-like material that can repair itself if it becomes damaged. After developing on the seabed, the fully grown unit is fished out of the water, ready to be used as a house. The team envisage an entire 'forest' of housing units growing in the seabed. Once shipped to dry land, they can be stacked and clustered in different configurations to form entire towns clustered around an atoll.

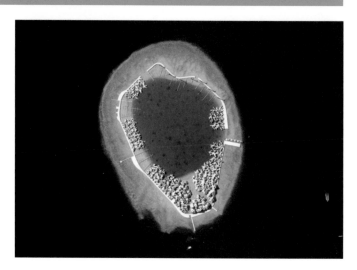

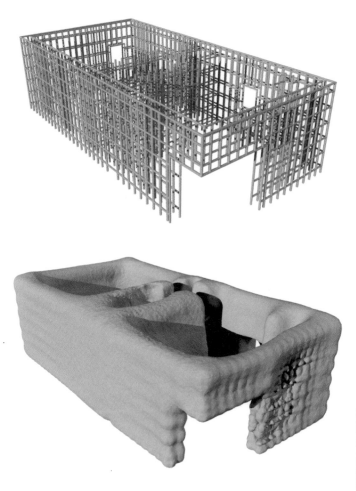

Studio Morison
Mother ..., 2020
Cambridgeshire, UK

Created specifically for a nature reserve in an area of wild fenland in rural Cambridgeshire, this project engages with the connections between our mental health and the natural world. The work was inspired by *Nature Cure* (2005) by Richard Mabey, in which the author recovers from severe depression by walking, watching and writing about the landscape of East Anglia. The timber used in the frame was felled from the artists' own forest and milled at their workshop. The thatched walls and roof, made from straw by a master thatcher, references local building traditions, materials and vernacular architecture, and the form itself is an interpretation of the hayricks once found dotted across this landscape. The artists note that the sculpture offers both a space for reflection and the opportunity to still the mind, while focusing on the simple material qualities of the work and the changing nature of its surroundings.

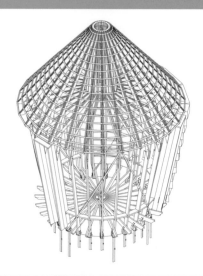

Redhouse Studio and NASA Institute for Advanced Concepts
Mars Habitat, 2018
Prototype

The myco-architecture project based at NASA's Ames Research Center in California is prototyping technologies to grow habitats on the Moon, Mars and beyond from fungi and the unseen underground threads that make up the main part of the fungus (mycelia). Ultimately, the aim is to allow human explorers to bring a compact habitat into space that will survive the journey. Under the proposal developed for creating a habitat on Mars, a lander vehicle will deliver the habitat package to the planet's surface. A rover vehicle meets the package and supplies it with carbon dioxide, nitrogen and water. The habitat inflates and unfolds, and its cells fill with water. Algae grows in the cells, and the algal biomass dehydrates. Mycelium consumes the algal biomass to create the composite material that forms the final structure, eventually creating a fully functional human habitat – all while being safely contained to avoid contaminating the Martian environment.

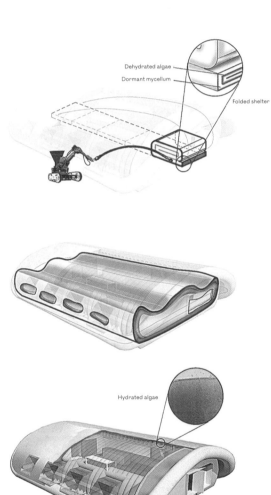

HARVEST

HARVEST
A holistic sense of place

Longstanding paradigms can shift if we reimagine energy as a resource to be borrowed and returned, rather than as the endpoint of a saleable transaction. This is the reshuffle proposed by the homes in this chapter. These are design strategies that reap the power of the wind, water and sun, but return the favour in the form of lowered CO_2 emissions, reduced site impact, a holistic sense of place, even crops of harvestable food for more than one species. The homes are inherently cyclical in character, mindful of the spaces they inhabit and try to avoid one-way ecological bargains.

The Covid-19 pandemic has demonstrated the fragility of the global supply-chain model. A localized model of responsible self-reliance is not only possible, but also carries benefits far beyond a single region. Passive houses are one step in this direction. For residents of 1301 New York Street House (p. 158), an LEED Platinum-certified passive house in Lawrence, Kansas, aiming for net zero translates into a monthly utility bill of about US$17, no small consequence in a region with extreme variations in temperature. A different but related approach resonates in the work of RicharDavidArchitekti, whose House with a Greenhouse (p. 158) is a low-energy brick home with a façade of larch planks, which helps to regulate air flow.

Soft-impact remote living is the aim of Aleksi Hautamäki and Milla Selkimäki, which is why they chose to power their self-sufficient weekend home with electricity from six solar panels connected to eight batteries, with a sauna stove providing all the heat (p. 159). It is also a motivating factor for Nice Architects, who design mobile micro-dwellings that can be used in virtually any setting (p. 160). In Denmark, a combination of sustainable housing development with afforestation offers a radical alternative to standard parcel and row housing and demonstrates circular resource thinking at the suburban and peri-urban levels (p. 161). Hong Kong-based architects Rural Urban Framework share this integrative approach, with projects that aim to restore ecological and economic balance in rural areas by helping to consciously evolve heritage with new knowledge and technologies from other parts of China (pp. 163, 164).

Studio 804
1301 New York Street House, 2015
Lawrence, Kansas, USA

Since its founding in 1995, Studio 804 has become known for socially responsible and sustainable design. It also offers a programme that gives students the chance to design and construct a building over the course of a year. To date, the team have built single-family homes, research centres and campus facilities. Three of their homes are Passivhaus certified. The goal with this project was to achieve a net-zero rating. The house is situated on an east–west axis for maximum solar gain, and photovoltaic tiles on the roof produce enough energy to counterbalance its consumption. A cut-out porch along the long southern façade helps block direct sunlight in summer to keep the house cool, three times the amount of insulation required was used to make it airtight. In a passive home, even the foundation slab and basement are insulated, with the increased costs of doing this recouped by energy savings. The team also chose sustainably harvested, durable and low-maintenance materials, including Alaskan Cedar shingles and a reflective metal roof that mitigates the heat-island effect.

RicharDavidArchitekti
House with a Greenhouse, 2018
Hořice, Czech Republic

The home – situated in the middle of an orchard to allow views of nature from all angles – is owned by a professional breeder of succulent plants. The architects designed the building with no particular hierarchy or main entrance. Rather, each room, regardless of function, is accessed directly from the wide porch wrapping around three sides of the house. The porch also plays a role in providing fresh air and cool interior temperatures. A single external staircase leads up to the rooftop greenhouse, covered by a large, overhanging translucent roof, made from polycarbonate, which lets in plenty of natural light and offers protection from the elements. The architects chose to place the greenhouse on top of the roof to maintain the expansive views and take advantage of the residual heat produced below.

Aleksi Hautamäki and Milla Selkimäki
Project Ö Cabin, 2019
Skjulskäret, Finland

The island of Skjulskäret is located at the edge of Finland's Archipelago National Park, home to a pine forest at the southern end and two rocky bays to the north. Before being purchased by Aleksi Hautamäki and Milla Selkimäki, it had never been inhabited. The pair built two small cabins at the northeast corner of the island, positioned close to the rocks below so that they blend in with their surroundings. Both buildings are completely self-sufficient, with solar power for electricity and a sauna stove for heat and hot water.

In the summer, solar panels produce enough energy for everything from lighting to the washing machine, with a generator used for additional power in the winter. A battery-free, solar-powered desalination system filters seawater to provide fresh water for drinking. Living off-grid requires extra effort to coordinate with natural forces. But, the couple notes, the peacefulness and fresh air instantly lower stress levels. The weather in the archipelago can change quickly, and a large part of the experience of living here is to plan the day according to wind directions and if it is cloudy, rainy or sunny. Every kind of weather, they add, has its own benefits.

Nice Architects
Ecocapsule, 2014
Bratislava, Slovakia

The idea for this smart micro-home began as a proposal for a design competition for small housing units on a ranch with no infrastructure. The team didn't win the competition, but unexpectedly received requests from people who wanted to purchase their design. In 2014, they produced the first prototype. Referencing the circular forms found in nature, the smooth elliptical form directs rainwater into a reservoir where it is purified with polypropylene and carbon filters. The unit also contains a composting toilet and energy-efficient LED lights. Its systems are monitored by a mobile app that also tracks weather conditions. Unlike an RV or mobile home, Ecocapsule doesn't drain power from campsite hosts, but instead harvests energy from a wind turbine and solar roof panels in combination with a high-capacity battery. Inside is a foldout bed and table, small kitchenette and working shower head.

Effekt
Naturbyen, 2020
Middelfart, Denmark

Effekt is an interdisciplinary team of designers, architects, urban planners, landscape architects and other specialists who take a holistic design approach to projects that resonate in local, regional and global contexts. *Effekt* is Danish for 'impact', and the group see themselves as thinkers and builders, believing that buildings and cities must create a lasting positive impact on people and the planet.

Denmark's current climate plan stipulates 70 per cent emissions reductions by 2030 and climate neutrality by 2050. As part of this, the National Forest Program has set an afforestation goal of no less than 20 per cent of the country's total area by 2100. For their Naturbyen masterplan, the architects consulted industry experts who advised an initial dense tree-planting, creating a micro-climate that would stimulate growth at an accelerated rate of fifteen years, rather than one hundred. Once established, the trees can be thinned out, and sublayers of vegetation introduced to increase biodiversity.

The homes will be built from natural and recyclable materials, primarily wood. Each cluster of homes is grouped in a circle around a central shared courtyard. To ensure a mix of residents as diverse as the forest, there are a number of home typologies and ownership models, including rental, cooperative and community units.

Rural Urban Framework
Jintai Village Reconstruction, 2017
Bazhong, China

The village of Jintai in Sichuan Province was hit hard by the Wenchuan earthquake on 12 May 2008, with nearly five million people left homeless. Although reconstruction efforts took place in the aftermath, heavy rainfall and landslides in 2011 again destroyed many of the newly built homes and locals were left with no further aid. This reconstruction project by Rural Urban Framework was completed with the support of the local government and NGOs. Comprising twenty-two houses and a community centre, the complex features four different housing types and implements a variety of new technologies that encourage self-sufficiency within a model of interdependency. These include green roofs, water collection and biogas facilities, along with reedbed waste treatment. The design also provides room for the communal rearing of pigs and chickens. All ground-level spaces are shared by the community as a whole. Architects John Lin and Joshua Bolchover are firm believers in infrastructure, and their practice tries to 'anticipate the urban while adding in what has been left out of the urbanization of the rural'.[32]

Rural Urban Framework
A House for All Seasons, 2012
Shijiazhuang, China

A House for All Seasons is in the village of Shijia in northwestern China, an area that has shifted gradually away from economic self-reliance as greater numbers of residents move to the cities to work and become increasingly dependent on imported labour and materials. The architects have proposed a sustainable contemporary prototype that reinstates a more independent model of living. The house is a network of interlocking parts, with the use of rammed earth, rainwater storage, reedbed water purification and biogas ensuring that energy gained in one area is converted for use in another. The design takes its cue from the traditional mud-brick houses of the region, updated with more efficient and sustainable technologies. Rooms are situated around four courtyards to encourage the flow of movement and air. The stepped roof looks like a sculpture park or playground, and invites residents to explore. In this new type of hybrid rural living, old and new can coexist. The house is also used as a centre for traditional straw weaving, helping to conserve the values of the location, bolster the local economy and cement the village identity for future generations.

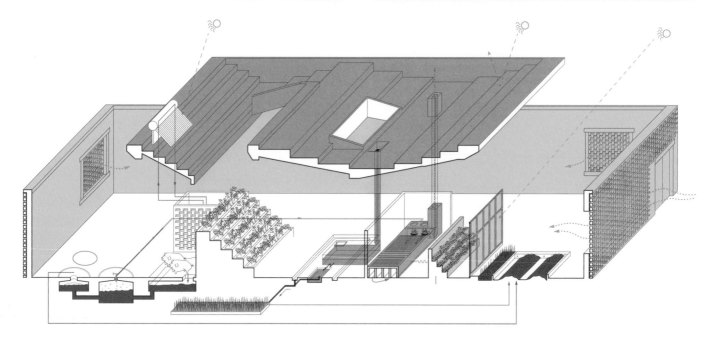

Patrick Nadeau
La Maison-vague, 2011
Reims, France

Patrick Nadeau is a pioneer of vegetal design, whose large-scale projects incorporate living plants as renewable material. La Maison-vague (Wave House) is a low-cost, single-family home in Sillery, near Reims, which owes its high thermal performance to a vegetal roof. Designed in collaboration with Pierre Georgel of Ecovégétal, the roof contains a mixture of grasses, sedums, thyme, lavender and other perennials, which both help regulate the house's interior temperature year round and have wider-ranging implications for the environment. It also provides a habitat for insects, which pollinate plants, disperse seeds, tidy up waste, and are themselves a protein-rich food stuff. Their populations are diminishing worldwide, however, due to the use of fertilizers and pesticides, as well as the degradation of natural habitats by monocultures. So in addition to providing its owners with a temperate indoor climate, herbs and flowers, and a place to gather, the house also participates in the ecological regeneration of its site.

BMDesign Studios
Concave Roof System, 2019
Jiroft, Iran

Global warming is reducing rainfall worldwide, and is of particular concern to inhabitants of arid countries with already low levels of precipitation. In Iran, the amount of rainfall is less than a third of the global average, with a rate of evaporation that is three times greater. BMDesign came up with a system that harvests potable water from an infinite resource (the atmosphere), rather than from already strained rivers, lakes and reservoirs. The idea is simple and direct: a system of nesting bowls is placed on top of courtyard homes and other civic buildings, which have smooth surfaces to help tiny droplets of rainwater merge into larger drops that can be collected and used. The architects want their design to be both visually pleasing and able to be applied at different scales and in different environments.

A HOLISTIC SENSE OF PLACE

PRESERVE

PRESERVE
Embrace what you've got

Demolishing buildings is a waste. As the projects in this chapter demonstrate, dilapidated, pre-loved structures have the potential to be rescued and reinvented, even when they resemble little more than a heap of rubble. Preserving all or part of an existing building gives it a longer life and makes the most of the energy and resources that went into making it. Reusing existing buildings also reduces the need to dispose of materials that might otherwise end up in landfill.

To create Croft Lodge Studio (p. 170), architect Kate Darby and designer David Connor took the remains of an eighteenth-century oak-framed cottage, stabilized it, and then wrapped it in an insulated casing of corrugated iron. Driven by the poetry and romance of the idea, they chose to preserve the cottage as it was – complete with overgrown ivy, cables, cobwebs and old bird's nests – and transform it into an office with guest accommodation, which could then be easily transformed back into a three-bedroom house.

House No 7 (p. 171) was the first in a trio of homes designed by Denizen Works in the Scottish Hebrides, built on the site of a ruined black house, a traditional low-profile cottage with thick stone walls, with techniques that date back thousands of years. The architects drew on the materials and forms of the island's agricultural buildings to create a family home, guest house and utility space. The guest house sits within the stone of the original cottage, with the main house and utility area extending from it to resemble a group of agricultural sheds around a sheltered garden.

Transforming rundown old buildings presents a unique set of challenges, especially when they are in overcrowded urban settings. The disorderly mishmash of buildings in Beijing's *hutongs* provided the inspiration for the Plugin House system by People's Architecture Office (pp. 171, 172). The architects developed the concept after the local authority issued a call for ideas about how the area could be upgraded, rather than bulldozed and rebuilt. The Plugin system is based on structurally insulated panels that slot together to create new, weathertight units, which are then installed inside existing buildings to upgrade the living standards without the need to rebuild.

**Kate Darby Architects and
David Connor Design
Croft Lodge Studio, 2017
Herefordshire, UK**

Kate Darby and David Connor's strategy for this 300-year-old listed cottage was not to renovate or repair it, but to preserve it perfectly, including rotten timbers, dead plants, bird's nests, cobwebs and dust. A steel frame was erected over the cottage, then infilled with timber, sheeted with orientated strand board (OSB), wrapped in a waterproof membrane, and finally clad in black corrugated iron.

In the new part of the building, the staircase was built by a local metalwork fabricator – one of the few components to be custom-made. Nearly everything else is a standard product. Every part of the old cottage has been used, with gaping holes and peeling plasterwork revealing different layers of the original fabric. Members of

historical societies have visited to study the preserved remnants as part of research into 18th-century construction methods and materials. The large chimney is the only part of the old building that protrudes into the new exterior. It was saturated when work began, and took about two years to fully dry out. The new outer shell is highly insulated and airtight, with double- and triple-glazed windows, and heating provided by a pair of wood-burning stoves. Electricity is supplied by photovoltaic panels on the south-facing roof. Kitchen units from Ikea are wrapped in sheets of stainless steel. The bathroom and hot-water cylinder are cleverly concealed behind panels that run along the first-floor mezzanine.

The couple note that each morning they find bits of the old building have flaked off onto the table. But they have a policy of only cleaning the new parts of the home, which makes the job much easier.

Denizen Works
House No 7, 2013
Isle of Tiree, Scotland, UK

Like most places on Tiree, the site is very exposed, with no land mass or vegetation to shelter it from the wind. The architects wanted to create a design that gave the house some protection from the wind, but allowed in plenty of natural light for warmth. The guest house is built in the stone from the original cottage and has two bedrooms, a bathroom and a living room. Behind the guest house, the main house has a large bedroom sunk into the landscape with a living room, kitchen and dining area above. The exterior resembles an agricultural building with its curved roof and corrugated panelling. A utility space, which also resembles an outbuilding, links the two parts of the house together.

People's Architecture Office
Courtyard House Plugin, 2014
Beijing, China

This project was a response to a call for ideas for upgrading Dashilar, a historic neighbourhood in the centre of Beijing, characterized by narrow alleys, or *hutongs*, and courtyard houses with little or no insulation. The area also has limited infrastructure and no sewage lines. The team developed a system of prefabricated structural panels that incorporated insulation, wiring, plumbing, doors, windows and finishes into one moulded part, were inexpensive to ship, easy to handle and locked together with a single hex wrench.

An entire home can be assembled by a few people in one day, with no special skills or training required, at a cost of about half of a standard renovation and a fifth of building a new courtyard house from scratch. The houses can be customized for different sites, with walls that open by sliding or tilting. In just one year, the project grew from an experimental prototype to a systematic solution with the potential to be applied across Dashilar.

**People's Architecture Office
Mrs Fan's Plugin House, 2016
Beijing, China**

Mrs Fan was born and raised in the Changchun Jie neighbourhood in the centre of Beijing, but her family moved to the suburbs when she was in high school. She turned to a Plugin House when she wanted to move back to her old close-knit neighbourhood. The new home replaces a section of the old house and adds new functions, including a kitchen and bathroom. The area has no sewage system, so a composting toilet was integrated into the design to provide a private bathroom. The living-room ceiling extends upwards to provide a double-height space with skylights on either side. The form is not defined by limitations imposed by building regulations, but by demands from the neighbours, as the house cannot block sunlight, air circulation or views. Even as the house was built, new demands were being put forward. The use of prefab structural panels, however, makes accommodating these changes simple, as removing entire sections of the building can be done on site.

**People's Architecture Office
Shangwei Plugin Houses, 2018
Shenzhen, China**

The rapid urban expansion of nearby Shenzhen engulfed villages like Shangwei, surrounding them with new developments. Houses, some of them hundreds of years old, were left abandoned for decades. The local authority must renovate uninhabitable properties where the roofs have collapsed, but this is difficult to achieve as any work would affect neighbouring buildings. The team gets round this problem by inserting a new structure within the existing house, leaving the original structure untouched.

Because some of the roof remained untouched, the Huang Family Plugin House acted as reinforcement for any structural problems the old building might have had. To add additional space, a bedroom was placed on the mezzanine level with a corner window cantilevering over a collapsed wall, offering a panoramic view of the village roofline. The slightly larger Fang Family house features a high window to bring southern light into the bedroom area at the rear of the house. For both homes, the system raises living standards by adding efficient mini-split units for heating and cooling, modern kitchens and off-grid composting toilets.

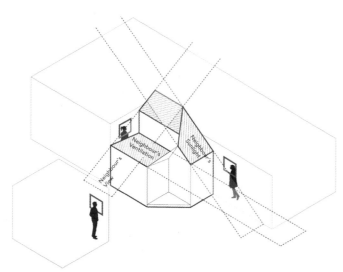

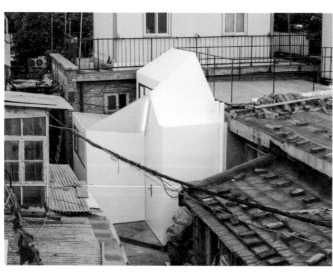

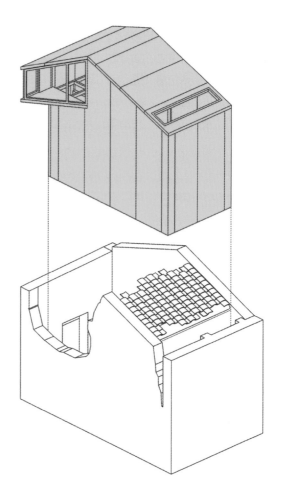

EMBRACE WHAT YOU'VE GOT

Tagarro-de Miguel Arquitectos
Casa Sabugo, 2013
Luarca, Spain

For this house in rural Spain, Tagarro-de Miguel Arquitectos demolished the gable wall of a modest cottage to open it up to the landscape. The house had been in the client's family for some time, and he had fond memories of playing there as a child. Inside, it was dark and cut off from the nearby sea and mountains. The team added steel and glass to contrast with the existing stone and timber, but left many imperfections and allowed the steel to weather and stain the walls.

'The house needed to breathe, so we gave it light, air and sea, but respected its essence, its past, its memory,' they note. 'The work had a lot of randomness and learning how to look, lots of madness and hopes, and quite a bit of thinking alongside a fantastic and sensitive client, who is really looking forward to a swing that will hang from the roof in front of the torn-down wall, in the same spot where he used to play as a kid.'

Bureau
Mr Barrett's House, 2019
Geneva, Switzerland

Architect Daniel Zamarbide of Bureau lifted a wooden alpine chalet from its concrete garage basement and overhauled the interior, before putting it back together. He compares the process to a surgical procedure, starting with the inside and working outwards. The house was designed for the fictional Hugo Barrett, a butler who manipulates and brings down his master in the film *The Servant* (1963). Much of the story takes place in a disorientating and claustrophobic Chelsea townhouse, with many scenes reflected in convex mirrors, like the large, porthole windows Zamarbide used to puncture the concrete walls. From the outside, the house looks like two unconnected layers, built at different times, using different materials in different styles. Inside, however, it is a unified and intricate arrangement of irregular spaces.

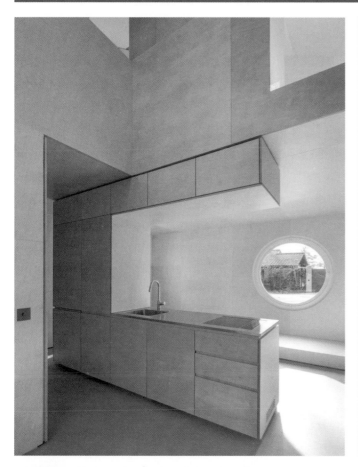

EMBRACE WHAT YOU'VE GOT

PRINT

PRINT
Housing at the touch of a button

Conventional homebuilding is wasteful. Next time you pass a construction site, look at the skips full of bricks and cement, offcuts and plasterboard. Building methods and materials in this multi-billion-pound industry haven't changed much over the last several centuries, and advocates of 3D-printing believe it's time they did. By taking an imaginative and altruistic approach, the creative teams included here demonstrate this relatively new technology's potential to build homes faster, cheaper and with less waste – both on and off the Earth.

Dmitri Julius of construction technologies company Icon believes a revolution in the homebuilding industry is long overdue. Icon built the first permitted 3D-printed home in the US in 2018 (p. 180), one of a series of shelters for homeless people in Austin, Texas. Since then, they have built homes for a community in Tabasco, Mexico (p. 181) and shelters for the US military, and are developing a printed lunar habitat for NASA. For Project Olympus (p. 181), an off-Earth construction system, the architects teamed up with Bjarke Ingels Group and SeARCH to develop prototype elements for a system that could print on the lunar surface, using moon dust as the main raw material.

Ideas that make it possible for people to live on other planets can also be applied to help us take better care of our own. With limited space and resources on the Moon and Mars, everything must be used and reused more efficiently. Emerging Objects turned to onsite materials for an experimental house in the San Luis Valley, Colorado, printed at the height of the Covid-19 pandemic (p. 183). WASP, a 3D-printing company based in Italy, are also making prototype houses using materials available onsite. The team collaborated with Mario Cucinella Architects to develop TECLA (p. 185), a pair of interconnecting domes that were 3D-printed using raw earth. Architect Massimo Moretti of WASP envisages a world where small technologically advanced, self-sufficient communities are built on a human scale, using onsite materials to make biodegradable buildings. 'Non-biodegradable parts are made from recyclable materials and can be reused indefinitely,' he says. 'All of this is already possible using a technology that can form a house by pressing a button.'

Icon
Chicon House, 2018
Austin, Texas, USA

Built in partnership with housing non-profit New Story, Chicon House is a prototype home designed with the developing world in mind, where power, water and building supplies are often inconsistent. It is the first permitted 3D-printed home in the US, and features two bedrooms, one bathroom and a kitchen area, surrounded by a large covered porch. A computer-controlled printer lays down layers, or 'beads', of Lavacrete, a quick-drying, cement-based mix, to form the internal and external walls, leaving gaps for windows, doors and utilities. A simple change to the coding that steers the printer results in a different arrangement, ensuring that each home is unique.

Icon
Community First! Village, 2020
Austin, Texas, USA

This series of 3D-printed homes for the homeless was created in partnership with the non-profit organization Mobile Loaves and Fishes, with architectural designs by Logan Architecture and finishings supplied by Franklin Alan, a local building firm. Each home has a bedroom, bathroom, kitchen, living room and large porch.

'We can print twenty-five houses in a row, and they can all be individual with a simple change to a few lines of code,' says Dmitri Julius of Icon. 'We are currently only limited by our imaginations. Beyond that, the machine's height dictates that we print single-storey homes, but designs for two-storey printers are in the pipeline.'[33]

Icon
New Story Project, 2019
Tabasco, Mexico

For this series of homes in the village of Tabasco, Mexico, Icon again teamed up with New Story to deliver shelter for families living in extreme poverty. Each home was printed in around twenty-four hours across several days, and features two bedrooms, a living room, kitchen and bath. They were designed according to feedback from the residents and built by Échale, New Story's partner in Mexico. Eventually, the village will include ten printed homes, along with dozens of others.

'Our long-term vision is thousands of Icon machines building tens of thousands of homes at scale worldwide,' Julius says. 'The global human housing issues are only increasing in complexity and volume. We need to work upstream against the factors that got us here to solve this problem – a scale solution for a scale problem.'[34]

Icon
Project Olympus, 2020
Prototype

Icon teamed up with the Bjarke Ingels Group (pp. 134, 187) and SeARCH (pp. 50, 182) to test, design and develop prototype elements for a full-scale 3D-printing system to build infrastructure on the Moon. In partnership with the NASA Marshall Space Flight Center in Huntsville, Alabama, it is testing lunar soil simulant with various processing and printing technologies.

'The opportunity to work with some of the best in their respective fields is always humbling,' Julius notes. 'We know our space, and they know theirs. All of the lessons learned from our projects pay dividends on others. Our teams cross-pollinate quite often, and we try to implement design breakthroughs in software, control systems and hardware across our product suites. I believe we will continue to learn lessons from Project Olympus, and apply them to our housing efforts and beyond.'[35]

SeARCH
Mars X-House V1 and V2
Prototype

'The projects we've been working on all use in-situ materials – moon dust or Martian dirt (regolith) – as the cost of bringing materials with us into space would be prohibitive,' says SeARCH co-founder Rebeccah Pailes-Friedman. 'The 3D-printing process is still under development, but will probably use laser-sintering or microwave-sintering. Both methods use solar energy to melt the regolith into a lava-like consistency, and then deposit it in layers to build a habitat. It is challenging and exhilarating to design for an environment we can only imagine living in. It forces us to reconsider everything – from how we move and live in a space to how we appropriate materials. Many aspects of our work have applications that are relevant to living and building on our own planet, especially in light of its dwindling raw materials and growing population.' [36]

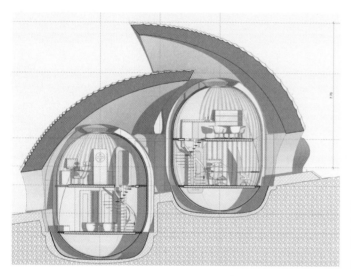

Emerging Objects
Casa Covida, 2020
San Luis Valley, Colorado, USA

This house for co-habitation in the time of Covid is an experiment in combining 3D-printing with local and traditional building materials, employing new and ancient ways of living. Located in the high alpine desert of the San Luis Valley, the case-study home is built with adobe, the traditional building material of the region, and is designed for two people to sleep, eat, bathe and gather together around the fire, with openings to the sky, the landscape and the ground. The sleeping platform, doors and lintels are made from locally harvested pine killed or damaged by the mountain pine beetle. An inflatable roof provides shelter from rain or snow and keeps in heat from the hearth.

Emerging Objects
Cabin of 3D-Printed Curiosities, 2018
Oakland, California, USA

An easing of Oakland's planning laws allowed the designers to build a garden cabin for showcasing some of their experiments in 3D-printing. Tiles feature throughout the design, including the ceramic tiles used for cladding the roof and sides of the house. Beads of 3D-printed clay create a loopy texture resembling scattered seeds, giving the tiles the appearance of having been knitted. Outside, an array of hexagonal planter tiles provides a living wall of succulents. For the interior, the team used translucent tiles made from a bioplastic derived from corn with LED lights positioned behind them.

'The cabin demonstrates that 3D-printing can be beautiful, meaningful and well crafted, rather than crude, fast and cheap,' note the architects.[37]

WASP
TECLA, 2021
Massa Lombarda, Italy

This prototype housing model printed entirely from earth and inspired by ancient building techniques is the result of a collaboration between WASP and Mario Cucinella Architects.

'It is an innovative circular housing model bringing together research on vernacular construction practices, the study of bioclimatic principles and the use of natural and local materials,' note the team, who describe TECLA as 'a pioneering example of low-carbon housing'.[38] It is a nearly zero-emission project, and the use of a local material allowed for the reduction of waste and scraps.

Founder Massimo Moretti adds: 'The limits placed on technology are mainly cultural. We need to rethink a large part of the current construction process, and imagine different aesthetics, shapes and surface finishes.'[39]

WASP
Gaia House, 2018
Massa Lombarda, Italy

This prototype dwelling was printed using raw earth as the main binding material, along with waste materials including straw and husks from rice production. Vegetable fibres were supplied by WASP's collaborator RiceHouse and used by the designers to develop a compound comprising 25 per cent soil taken from the site (30 per cent clay, 40 per cent silt and 30 per cent sand), 40 per cent straw and chopped rice, 25 per cent rice husk and 10 per cent hydraulic lime.

'The kind of building we propose is not a house that imposes itself by destroying the environment, but one that coexists with it in harmony and accepts the cycles of time,' says Massimo Moretti. 'A house that has a negative CO_2 load.'[40]

Bjarke Ingels Group
Mars Science City, 2017
Dubai, United Arab Emirates

This proposal is a hybrid of three approaches to protect people from the extreme environment on Mars: excavating, 3D-printing and inflating. A combination of tunnels, caves and structures printed with the excavated regolith will sit beneath the protection of an inflatable dome. The project has evolved from a single dome to groups of fused domes in a ring, which will eventually house one million people.

At Mars Science City, a space centre planned for a desert site outside Dubai, the designers tested and adapted their ideas. 'We wanted to explore what a Martian vernacular would look like,' the team notes. 'Designing for low gravity, low pressure, extreme cold and high levels of radiation radically changes the architect's tool kit and the resulting forms and spaces.'[41]

With limited resources on Mars, everything must be used and reused more efficiently. 'One of the main reasons behind global warming on Earth is fossil fuels,' says founder Bjarke Ingels. 'On Mars, there are no fossil fuels because there are no fossils. The systems and principles that will allow us to live on Mars are the same as those that allow us to be great custodians on Earth.'[42]

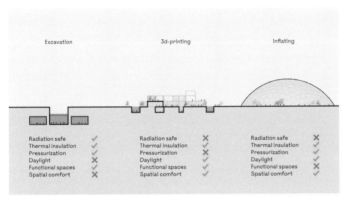

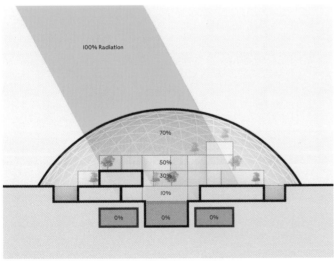

REUSE

REUSE
It's only waste if we waste it

Toothbrushes: millions are made worldwide each year. They are strong, durable, and will outlast us by hundreds of years. But like thousands of other consumables, we only use them for a short time before throwing them away. When you consider all of the things we regularly toss in the bin and forget about (in the UK, about half a ton a year per person), getting rid of it all mounts up to a massive global problem. But does it have to be?

The projects included here challenge our perception of waste. Duncan Baker-Brown and students at the University of Brighton repurposed over 19,800 unwanted toothbrushes as insulation for their pioneering Brighton Waste House (p. 192). In Australia, Alexander Symes also used salvaged materials for his fun mishmash of a three-bedroom house (p. 192). For Cubo House (p. 194), Phooey Architects applied the Surrealist technique of Cubomania, cutting up demolition drawings and then rearranging them to come up with a design for the new extension. And in Portland, Oregon, Julia Mollner of the Center for Public Interest Design set up the Useful Waste Initiative (p. 196) to divert construction materials from landfill and put them to good use.

Since few of us have access to designers with the vision and skills to transform waste into buildings, how can reusing waste be scaled up to make a bigger difference? With around 750 million tonnes of construction and demolition waste (CDW) produced each year in Europe alone, designers and entrepreneurs are investigating ways of processing it into building materials. In Rotterdam, Ferry in 't Veld and Nina Aalbers of Architectuur Maken designed their own home using construction waste bricks (p. 196), while the open-source network Precious Plastic provides plans and designs for machines and products that recycle plastic (p. 197). CDW is also the focus of the research project RE4 (p. 197), which developed a prefabricated, energy-efficient building concept made mostly from waste. When companies that want to introduce recycled materials do not have to make expensive changes to their production processes, the industrialization of these technologies becomes sustainable, both environmentally and economically.

BakerBrown
Brighton Waste House, 2014
Brighton, East Sussex, UK

Over 85 per cent of the materials used in this project came from building sites and household waste. Toothbrushes, denim offcuts and thousands of VHS tapes, floppy disks and DVD cases were repurposed as insulation, with discarded inner tubes, carpet tiles, reclaimed timber and plywood, vinyl banners, old ship lights, a discarded kitchen, damaged plasterboard and pieces of MDF also used in the design.

The low-energy building was created in partnership with recycling charity Freegle, housing and social-care provider Mears Group, Greater Brighton Metropolitan College and a range of specialists and waste-concern enterprises. It is now a research workshop for university staff and students. Architect Duncan Baker-Brown notes that through an innovative and collaborative design process, the team has made waste look good – crucial, he points out, since many people think that projects made from rubbish look like a pile of rubbish.

Alexander Symes Architect
Up-Cycle House, 2017
Blackheath, New South Wales, Australia

Instead of carting away the debris from a redundant house that previously stood on the site, the architect retained as much of it as possible to build his new home. Any new elements were made from recycled materials, resulting in a sustainable, functional and comfortable home that delights in its unique and fragmented form.

Up-Cycle House is a site for experimentation and pushing the limits of what is possible with bricolage in housebuilding. It comprises three bedrooms, two bathrooms and a generous open-plan living/dining/kitchen area. Entry is via a 'solar pergola', which provides shelter and generates 1 kw of energy from photovoltaic cells. Internally, salvaged tiles, recycled windows and reclaimed timber give the house a consistent look. Outside, the garden has been shaped by old railway sleepers and reused bricks.

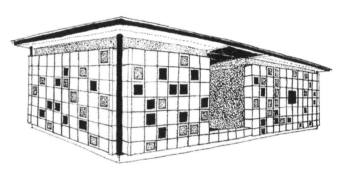

**Phooey Architects
Cubo House, 2013
Melbourne, Australia**

Using the Surrealist technique of Cubomania to catalogue, reuse and reinvent materials from a demolished building, the team placed a grid over photographs of the old house, cut them up and rearranged them for the new design. Materials and offcuts from the former building were salvaged and upcycled without disguising their original purpose, with security screens reassembled to provide shade and privacy for a new rear window. Leftover balustrades were used as a screen for a loft bed and handles in the kitchen. Slate roof tiles became windowsills, and a chandelier was made from an old staircase. The team also applied a pattern of recycled bricks to the outside of the new extension, carrying it into the floor and walls of the garden, designed in collaboration with Simon Ellis Landscape Architects.

Center for Public Interest Design
Useful Waste Initiative, 2016
Portland, Oregon, USA

Mock-ups play an important role in the construction industry, and are used for performing tests, understanding material compatibility and demonstrating design aesthetics. Although costly, they are often discarded after use. Julia Mollner of the Center for Public Interest Design, however, saw that with a few adjustments they could be diverted from landfill and used as micro-dwellings in Oregon's houseless villages. She liaised with architects and contractors and produced a guidebook specifying how to build mock-ups so they can be repurposed. Given the cost of disposal, it makes financial sense to use, rather than dump them. Even the most basic mock-ups, with just a few walls, can be reused by dismantling them for structural components or materials, or converting them into fully enclosed structures.

Architectuur Maken
De Gouverneur, 2016
Rotterdam, Netherlands

This narrow house in Rotterdam might look like its neighbours, but its bricks are made from compacted construction waste. Although the city is dense, there are empty plots in the centre and the local authority is encouraging their development. This four-storey infill house is built on a small plot, 4.7 m (15 ft) wide by 8.8 m (29 ft) deep. Architects Ferry in 't Veld and Nina Aalbers chose to build with recycled bricks, which complement the surrounding buildings, from Dutch startup StoneCycling – the first time its bricks have been used at this scale.

'A mix of brick bonds is used, in which the sliced stones form long vertical lines across the façade,' note the manufacturers. 'These sliced stones show the materials used: building waste, such as glass; ceramic waste, such as toilet bowls and roof tiles. So the waste provides the decoration in the façade and is at the same time identifiable, showing the beauty of a circular building material.'

Precious Plastic
Extruded Plastic Bricks, 2019
Eindhoven, Netherlands

Precious Plastic is an open-source network for tackling the plastic waste problem. It's a combination of people, machines, platforms and knowledge, all of which come together to create an alternative global recycling system. Members gather plastic in their community and take it to collection points. Once the plastic is shredded, it can be transformed at one of the project's workspaces into something new, including benches, stools, bicycle pedals, even a boat. All of the information, code, drawings and source material is freely available online. Extruded plastic bricks, beams and tiles are just some of the products people can make from their 'how-to' packs. As well as instructions on how to put together moulds and make the bricks, Precious Plastic also provide guides to making small structures such as bike sheds.

RE4 Project
Demos, 2016–20
Madrid, Spain; Benevento, Italy; Toomebridge, UK

How do you recycle a whole building? The RE4 Project set out to develop a method of using CDW as the source material for energy-efficient prefabricated building components. These components also had to be easy to put together and take apart, so they could be used again and again. One of the early challenges was to develop a new way of sorting and processing waste materials on construction sites, from roof tiles to bricks, concrete and plastics. The team developed a prototype robot that separates and classifies different types of waste as it passes along a conveyor built. After sorting, the waste is used to make items such as concrete beams and panels, insulated timber façades and partitions. These are designed so they can be disassembled once the building is no longer needed. So far, the project has seen demonstration homes built in Spain, Italy and the UK to test the performance of the materials in different climates.

REVISIT

REVISIT
Just like starting over

We don't need to look further than our own backyards for advice on constructing sturdy and healthy homes. There is wisdom to be found in centuries-old traditions of building that still work. The designers in this chapter have chosen to take the long view, reconnecting to local knowledge and empirical methods that used to be handed down from generation to generation. With a few technological tweaks, they have updated tried-and-true approaches to show that 'continuity' and 'change' need not be mutually exclusive terms.

Bumpers Oast House (p. 202) is the result of in-depth research into the oast houses that are common to Kent in the UK. For their 21st-century interpretation, the team at ACME based its proportions on the original, but used thick timber passive modules faced with peg tiles in place of solid brick walls. Self-taught builder Dennis Carter also prizes the timeless value of quality construction. Deer Isle Hostel in Maine (p. 203), completed over a period of seven years, takes it cues from American Colonial architecture found along the Eastern seaboard. Stéphanie Chalthiel of MuDD Architects approaches another traditional method – earth building – from a contemporary angle, using remote-controlled drones to spray fine layers of biomaterial onto lightweight structures (p. 204).

Thatching is another age-old craft that uses biomaterial to protect and weatherproof a house. Multidisciplinary firm Proarh used it to breathe new life into Hiža (p. 205), a historic cottage in the village of Kumrovec, Croatia. The research of architectural technologist Kathryn Larsen into the feasibility of eelgrass as a contemporary building material is inspired by the ancient practice of using it for thatching on the Danish island of Læsø. For her Seaweed Pavilion (p. 206), she integrated woven eelgrass panels into the structure. Søren Nielson of Vandkunsten Architects also used eelgrass for an experimental summer house on Læsø (p. 206), completed in 2013 as the winning entry of the Realdania Byg Foundation competition. But instead of wrapping the grass around a roof's rafters, with additional layers added as maintenance, he used machine-knitted tubes stuffed with eelgrass to insulate the entire non-treated wood home.

ACME
Bumpers Oast House, 2019
Kent, UK

This house is the result of in-depth research into the local vernacular of the 17th- and 18th-century oast houses that are common to this part of southeastern England. Many of these conical kiln buildings, originally used to dry hops for brewing, are still standing today, often repurposed as private homes. For their 21st-century interpretation, the architects based the proportions of the five tower roundels on those found in a traditional oast house, with all of the house's private functions stacked in the towers. The piled effect draws airs up through the building, in much the same way as it would have circulated in the original buildings. The transformation of old structures like oast houses is often possible, the team note, as many of them were designed with more ceiling height, bigger rooms and larger windows, allowing scope for adaptation. This allows buildings to grow and adapt to new uses over hundreds of years. Today, houses are designed to conform to minimum building regulations, and lack the flexibility to adapt over time. To be truly sustainable, they add, we need buildings designed with a 'loose' fit, to allow for several centuries of unpredictable reuse.

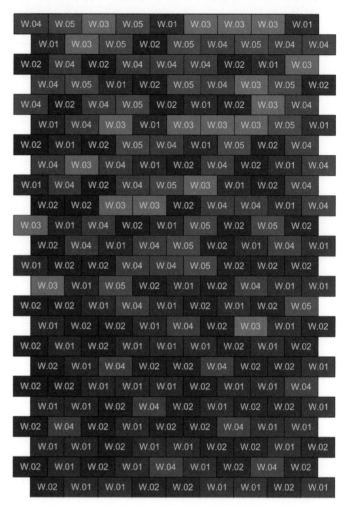

Dennis Carter and Anneli
Carter-Sundqvist
Deer Isle Hostel, 2009
Deer Isle, Maine, USA

'Some of the oldest housing stock
in the US can be found in Maine,
where the average age of a home is
100 years old,' says Dennis Carter,
an eleventh-generation resident of
the state. 'But today, very few people
understand how to preserve them.'[43]

Carter notes that his forebears
lived long and happy lives in timber-
framed homes (his grandparents'
house dates to 1778). He and his
wife Anneli view Deer Isle Hostel as
a successful demonstration of an
alternative economic system, with a
number of features that contribute
to its self-sufficiency, including a root
cellar for storing vegetables, drying
racks for plants, sawdust toilets, a
compost-heated shower, vegetable
gardens and an orchard.

The design was inspired by the
17th-century Bennett-Boardman
House in Saugus, Massachusetts,
which has a virtually intact interior.
With the aid of a professional timber-
framer and a copy of *Build a Classic
Timber-Framed House* by Jack. A.
Sabon, Carter carved the frame
using red spruce, which was already
on site, dug out the cellar himself and
split and laid granite stones acquired
from a local quarry. Using centuries-
old construction methods, including
mortise-and-tenon joints held
together with handmade pegs, he
then framed and boarded the house
entirely by hand.

**MuDD Architects
Mud Shell, 2018
Prototype**

Stéphanie Chalthiel began her career hand-building earth houses in Mexico and French Guyana. Since then, a Marie Curie scholarship has given her the means to pursue sustainable building techniques, using readily available technologies like drones to apply biomaterials onto lightweight domes and other structures. Her method puts a sustainable twist on shotcrete (pneumatically sprayed concrete or mortar), already in use in industrial building practice.

Together with her team, Chalthiel has experimented with high-tech drones that can carry up to 100 kg (220 lbs) of biomaterial, kept within aviation safety regulations in urban areas by large net cages. She has already received requests from clients interested in using the method to waterproof roofs or clean buildings. Long term, the method could help construct sustainable living spaces in urban areas, as the drones replace scaffolding, carry heavy material, are easy to transport and work quickly and efficiently. They could also contribute to retrofitting unhealthy façades or seeding vertical urban gardens.

Proarh
Hiža, 2015
Kumrovec, Croatia

Thatching helps direct droplets of water downwards so that the roof can dry quickly. Because it also provides good insulation and can be used in tropical or temperate climates, it is a method that is well worth revisiting. The team at Proarh chose it specifically because it breathes and changes with time, and creates a healthy living environment.

'The process itself is the same as in past centuries, using the same basic tools,' note the architects. 'Sustainability does not mean just following guidelines regarding energy-efficiency, renewable materials, upcycling, recycling, and so on. For us, it also represents an idea of respect.'[44]

As well as thatch, the home has well-insulated windows, underfloor heating and high-quality materials for ceilings and walls to ensure that no energy is wasted. An open fireplace for heating and cooking also helps keep the ground floor warm. 'This mix of traditional elements and construction solutions, based on centuries of experience, with contemporary building technologies is a good recipe for any region or design,' they add.

Studio Kathryn Larsen
The Seaweed Pavilion, 2019
Læsø Island, Denmark

Kathryn Larsen's Seaweed Pavilion was inspired by the communally built homes on the island of Læsø, covered with layers of eelgrass. Although eelgrass, which can last up to 400 years, is a naturally fireproof and well-insulating material, there has been resistance to using it in construction for fear that it might rot or smell. When properly prepared and dried, however, eelgrass is rot-resistant and smells like normal grass. Larsen's prototype panels can be used for insulation or acoustics, before being dissembled and reused or recycled, greatly reducing emissions when the building is demolished or moved. She links sustainability with understanding the impact of our actions on the planet, particularly the kinds of emissions caused by the construction industry. Eventually, she plans to publish the results of her findings in an open-source databank, making the information available to everyone.

Vandkunsten Architects
Modern Seaweed House, 2013
Læsø Island, Denmark

For their own experimental seaweed house on Læsø, Vandkunsten Architects used both an ancient material and a medieval method in a new way. The base structure, floors and interior are made entirely from low-impact wood, which serves as an immediately beneficial and necessary replacement for high-impact concrete. The roof and façade, however, take their cues from the old seaweed-thatched houses on the island. The team used industrial knitting machines to make long tubes, which they stuffed with eelgrass sourced from a seaweed bank. These were attached to the timber frame as insulation for the walls and floors, and to clad the roof and façade, as well as the ceiling. Substituting eelgrass for industrial materials cuts down CO_2 emissions and provides durable insulation. Ironically, it ended up being one of the costlier items – even though it is still possible to harvest eelgrass from the coast – because the craft has become so rare.

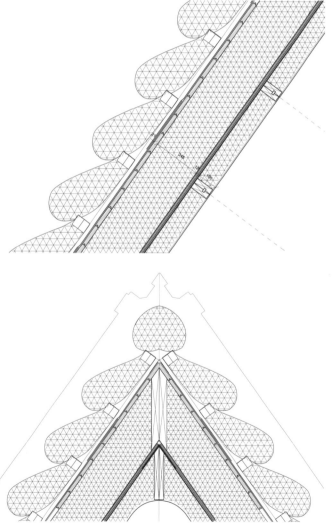

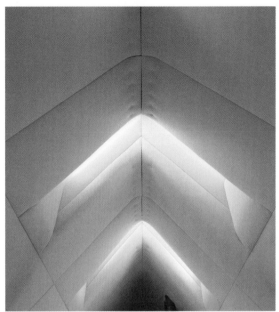

RISE

RISE
Let the waters come

Many cities sit on the bank of a river or estuary, and their relationship with their watery neighbours can be tense, especially in places where the fortifications built to keep water from valuable infrastructure and buildings is no longer up to the job. Do we build bigger defences and hope they hold back the floods for another few decades, retreat to higher ground, or – as the architects and engineers in this chapter propose – upgrade our building technology to let the water in?

After witnessing the devastation caused by Hurricane Katrina in New Orleans in 2005, Dr Elizabeth English of the Buoyant Foundations Project decided to explore solutions that would protect communities and homes from flooding. The group won its first major grant in 2016 to retrofit four rice farmers' houses in the Mekong River Delta in Vietnam (p. 212). The system is customized for different communities – as in the case of Casa Anfibia in Nicaragua (p. 212) – depending on need, available materials and climate.

H&P Architects employed a similar idea for Blooming Bamboo Home (p. 213) in Vietnam, a modular, self-assembled house that can withstand floods of up to 1.5 m (5 ft) deep. In the UK, the country's first amphibious house – Formosa (p. 216) by Baca Architects – can rise more than 2.5 m (8 ft) when it floods. Another option for building homes in flood-risk areas is to elevate them permanently, which Baca Architects did with Othello Way (p. 216), eleven flood-resilient homes in Stratford-upon-Avon, Warwickshire. The whole site is designed to flood, with landscaped areas that can store floodwater, slow its flow, and naturally filter it before it enters the main drainage system.

Also in the UK, DHaus elevated whole streets above the flood waters for an imaginative take on what London townhouses might look like in the year 2118. For a competition entry, they proposed building plywood replicas of pastel-coloured period terraced houses on top of flood-proof concrete plinths in Kentish Town, North London (p. 217). This playful take on the attractive Georgian houses found in pockets of the capitol will lift future Londoners above their submerged streets.

Buoyant Foundations Project
Amphibious Houses, 2018
Mekong River Delta, Vietnam

The team worked alongside local experts and community members to retrofit four houses in Vietnam's Mekong River Delta, supplementing the vernacular technique of elevating houses on stilts in this flood-prone region. Plastic barrels were fitted beneath the houses to help them float, and the homes themselves were anchored into place with a series of telescopic posts, which slide up and down as the floodwater level rises and falls. Team members from Canada coordinated the builds in An Giang and Long An provinces in 2018, with local partners monitoring the houses' performance during the flood season. At the end of the project, the team conducted post-flood interviews with the residents of the four test homes to gauge their satisfaction.

Buoyant Foundations Project
Casa Anfibia
Malacatoya, Nicaragua

The Buoyant Foundations system can be customized to different communities, depending on their needs, available materials and the local climate. For this home in Nicaragua, the project team surrounded the building with a deck, so that the family won't have to bring their pigs and chickens inside. Wherever the team works, the goal is to benefit people in need, while working with nature and letting the floodwater lift people to safety.

**Buoyant Foundations Project
Port Maria
Port Maria, Jamaica**

These diagrams of amphibious homes – proposed for the town of Port Maria in Jamaica, which is prone to severe seasonal flooding that causes significant damage to homes and health risks to residents –

show how the foundations work. Polystyrene blocks beneath the existing floor structure provide buoyancy, and a plywood structural substrate reinforces the building and supports the blocks. The vertical guidance system uses readily available timber telephone poles to prevent any lateral movement of the house as it rises, floats and descends.

**H&P Architects
Blooming Bamboo Home, 2013
Vietnam**

Vietnamese studio H&P Architects developed Blooming Bamboo Home as a modular, self-build house with a bamboo frame, which can be assembled by simply bolting, binding,

hanging and placing the different materials. The frame can be finished with readily available materials such as bamboo wattle, coconut leaf or fibreboard, with modules added to larger groups. The house is anchored to the ground with steel piles and sits on a pontoon made from recycled plastic drums.

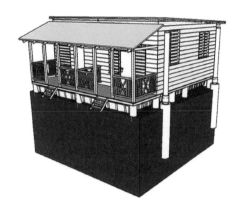

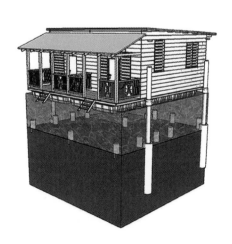

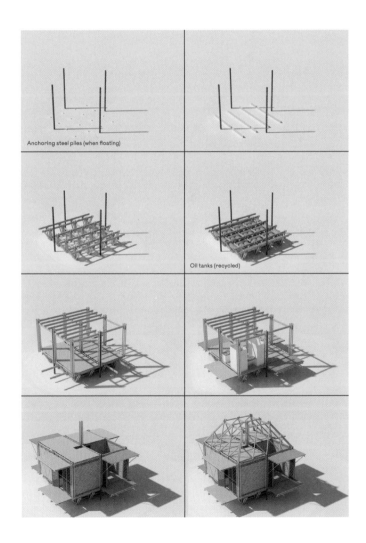

Baca Architects
Formosa, 2014
Marlow, Buckinghamshire, UK

Built on a small island in the River Thames, Formosa was the first amphibious home in the UK, sitting on a floating base that is nearly invisible from the outside. The floor is raised by less than 1 m (3 ft) above the ground, rather than the 2 m (7 ft) required if it was not amphibious. A carefully laid-out garden acts as a natural flood-warning system, with terraces set at different levels to flood incrementally and alert the occupants well before the flood water reaches threatening levels. The lowest terrace is planted with reeds, and the next one up with shrubs and plants. The lawn is next, with the highest point just beneath the living room. The levels improve recovery by providing dry areas as water levels drop and plants help to reduce saltation of the dock. The house is connected to its utilities via elephant cabling, flexible service pipes designed to extend up to 3 m (10 ft), allowing all the services to remain clean and operational during a flood. Crucially, this also allows the residents to return home immediately afterwards.

Baca Architects
Othello Way, 2021
Stratford-upon-Avon, Warwickshire, UK

Amphibious homes that rise with flooding can be expensive, and a cheaper option is to elevate them permanently. Here, a gently ramped road provides access from the middle of the site to the raised houses, which are elevated on stilts, while an elevated pedestrian and cycle path to the west provides a through-route and acts as a safe haven during flooding. Space is made for water across the site. The long-term goal, notes Baca director Richard Coutts, is to design communities that function as normal, preserving continuity of daily life during droughts and flooding.

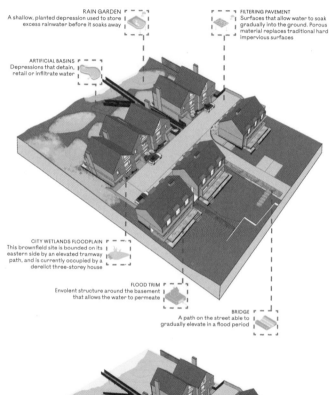

RAIN GARDEN
A shallow, planted depression used to store excess rainwater before it soaks away

FILTERING PAVEMENT
Surfaces that allow water to soak gradually into the ground. Porous material replaces traditional hard impervious surfaces

ARTIFICIAL BASINS
Depressions that detain, retail or infiltrate water

CITY WETLANDS FLOODPLAIN
This brownfield site is bounded on its eastern side by an elevated tramway path, and is currently occupied by a derelict three-storey house

FLOOD TRIM
Envolent structure around the basement that allows the water to permeate

BRIDGE
A path on the street able to gradually elevate in a flood period

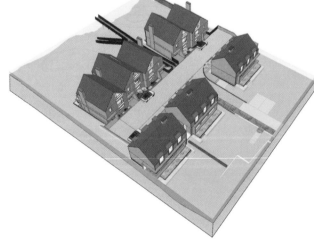

DHaus
The Kentish Classic, 2018
London, UK

Cut-out plywood replicas of period terrace houses are built on flood-proof concrete plinths in DHaus's Venetian take on Kentish Town, North London, in the 22nd century. The façades sit on top of 3D-printed platforms, sculpted like works of art. A flowing staircase curves in and out of the floors, linking them together to create double-height spaces. The staircase leads up to the third-floor roof garden, where residents can still have outside space during floods. The Kentish Classic is an homage to the colourful rows of houses found in parts of North and West London. Stained plywood is used to emulate the rainbow-effect street scene of the Georgian and Victorian terraced façades.

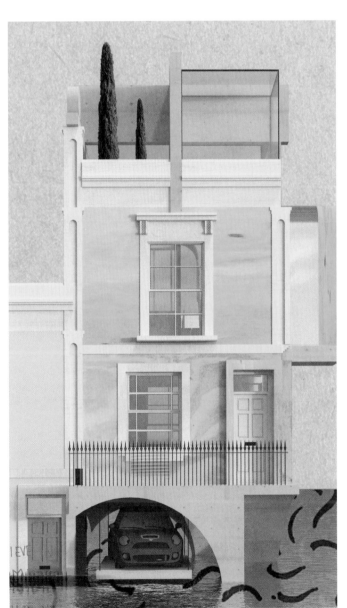

TRANSFORM

TRANSFORM
Anything can become something else

Farmyards and docklands are rich hunting grounds for architects and designers in search of industrial detritus to transform into something new. The projects in this chapter demand that we change our relationship with materials. Instead of extracting more natural resources and expending energy (and money) transporting and processing them, why not make better use of all this readily available 'stuff'? With a keen eye, some playful thinking and a bit of love, these objects can be given a new purpose. From shipping crates to grain silos, the big challenge is transforming containers originally designed for storing products into comfortable spaces for people.

Dutch studios Refunc and MUD Projects achieve this by ditching the drawing board and designing on the fly. They sketch and improvise with found objects and allow the materials to determine the design, as seen in Refunc's experimental home Silo House (p. 228) and the living pods and hideouts by Boris Duijneveld of MUD Projects (pp. 226, 227). The trick, Duijneveld says, is to take the object out of its old context. In Argentina, Martin Marro delved deep into the past by transforming an old diesel storage tank into a living capsule (p. 230), as part of an ongoing artistic exploration into memories of his family home, a former 1940s filling station in Luque, Argentina.

These projects are compact, but if you find bigger objects, you can make bigger buildings. JYA-Rchitects used shipping containers for a low-cost house they completed with the non-profit organization, ChildFund Korea. The team replaced a rat-infested, rundown home with three colourful containers, arranged to maximize space for a family of seven (p. 223). Using a similar idea was the Peruvian firm TRS Studio. For CN House (p. 223), the team used a pair of adapted shipping containers as a base, topped with a recycled timber frame and polycarbonate roof. Re Arquitectura also turned to shipping crates for a nature-loving family who wanted three low-impact, independent apartments for their sons in Santa Ana, Costa Rica (p. 222). And just because you come from the scrapheap doesn't mean you can't live the high life, as Edward van Vliet demonstrated with his overhaul of a derelict crane in Amsterdam (p. 231).

Re Arquitectura
Containers Franceschi, 2017
Santa Ana, Costa Rica

Built from old shipping containers, these three apartments in Santa Ana – a collaboration between the architects and DAO – were lifted off the ground to dispense with the need for extensive foundations, ground-level insulation and damp-proofing, and to allow the soil beneath to absorb rainwater. Offcuts from the containers were used to make planters and hangers to extend the character of the houses into the garden, and balconies face south, offering spectacular views towards the hills and the Uruca River canyon. Inside, mobile furniture, an alternating-tread staircase and customized storage create flexible and versatile compact spaces. The architects left markings such as the serial numbers and branding to show the containers' original purpose, and spare parts were used to make fittings such as handrails and door handles. Timber floors and cane screens help to soften the homes' industrial appearance and allow them to blend into the landscape.

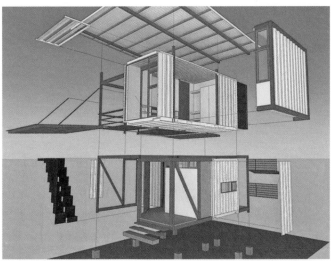

JYA-Rchitects
Low Cost House 2, 2013
Jangheung, South Korea

Low Cost House 2 is home to a family of seven near Jangheung, at the southern tip of South Korea. The shipping containers are separated with a wooden deck, and clear polycarbonate panels and wide sliding doors flood the space with light. Placing the containers inside a house-shaped frame creates more living space and an extra layer of insulation, and painting them bright yellow and pink softens their hard exterior. The yellow box houses the kitchen, toilets and washrooms, and the pink boxes contain the bedrooms. The home was built to replace an old, shabby building that tilted to one side and stood next to a cow shed. According to the architects, the worst part about the whole process was the rats: 'After examining the whole house, we decided to knock it down and rebuild it. It was clearly not in a condition to be renovated and, above all, it seemed the only way to escape from the rats.'[45]

TRS Studio
CN House, 2018
Callao, Peru

CN House is a proposal by TRS Studio to provide homes in Pachacutec, a marginalized, informal settlement in Callao, Peru, by pairing shipping containers. On the ground floor, they contain a living area, kitchen, bathroom, bedroom and indoor garden. Upstairs are more bedrooms and a bathroom, with a mezzanine office space. Large container doors extend the living space to the outdoors. A lightweight timber frame clad in recycled polycarbonate sheets sits on top of the containers, extending the available living space and providing plenty of natural light. The architects came up with a modular system to allow communities to work together to build their homes, which are designed to be flexible and moved to other locations as needed.

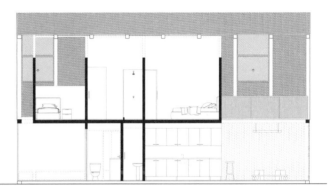

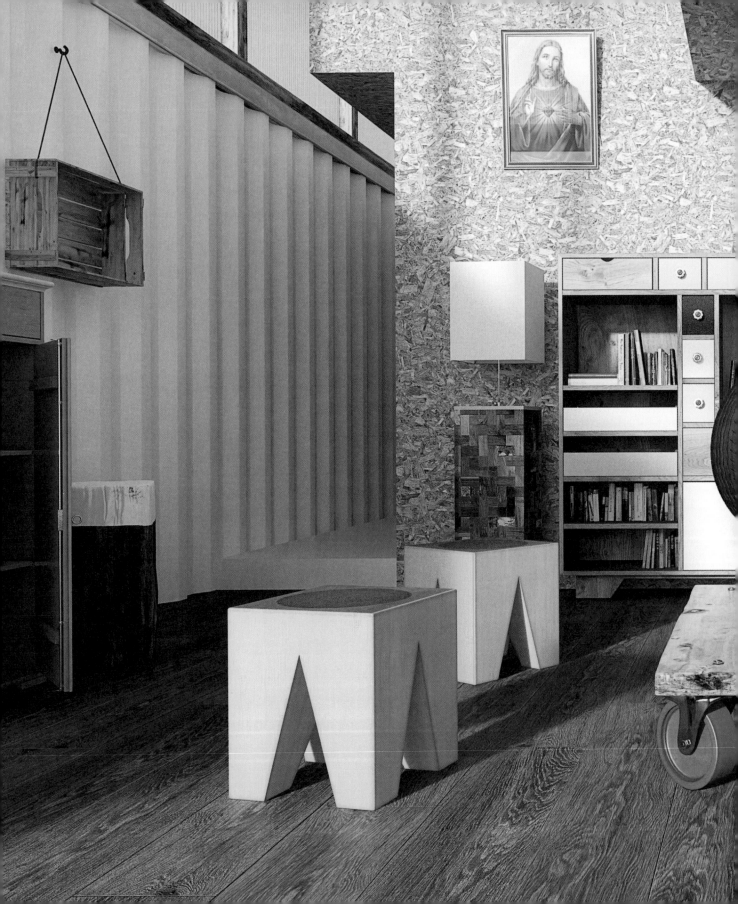

MUD Projects
Little Pea, 2013
Rotterdam, Netherlands

Culture Campsite, located in a disused car park in Rotterdam, offers sustainable camping within a green city oasis. Dutch firm MUD Projects was part of the team behind the concept, which allows visitors to experience staying in shelters made from waste architecture – in the case of Little Pea, discarded animal feed silos. It was originally designed as a mobile shelter, fitted to a pickup truck. Different pieces of the silos were assembled to create a self-sufficient living space, complete with a sofa, table, storage, heating and a kitchen with gas and running water.

MUD Projects
Cho, 2021
Rotterdam, Netherlands

The architects sketch and design with the materials and objects available. Playing with form, material and colour leads to new insights and shapes that couldn't be imagined on a sheet of paper. Working in this way requires a different way of designing to change, adapt and merge existing forms. As architect Boris Duijneveld notes, the project was called 'Cho' as it resembles a cocoon and *cho* is the symbolic name for a butterfly in Japanese. Taking five years to build, the unusual shape was created by fastening two discarded cattle-feed silos to an old plywood container.

Refunc
Silo House, 2013
The Hague, Netherlands

This mobile-house experiment, made from a 7 m (23 ft)-high, 2.4 m (8 ft)-diameter agricultural feed silo, is Dutch firm Refunc's first working example of vertical micro-architecture. Like life in a space station, onboard solutions are minimal and make a link to low-cost, energy-saving and small-footprint housing.

Construction took eight months, and Korbes says he learned a lot from living in a caravan for two years. Unlike his caravan, however, he wanted this new home to be suitable for four-season living.

'We want to inspire people to change their way of looking at the world,' he says. 'For us, there is no waste. Anything can become something else. There is no waste in nature. Look at everything you use or buy, and think about what you will do

with it after you've used it. There's a difference between end-of-use and end-of-life.'[46]

The floor area is 13 m² (140 sq ft), comprising a sleeping level, living space and kitchen, library and technical services, and provides accommodation for two people. Features include an airlock entrance, climbing wall, bathtub, dry toilet, basement library, panorama window, micro-balcony, rainwater system and garden units.

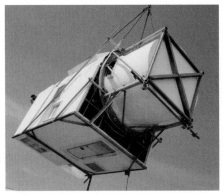

TRANSFORM

Martin Marro
Bunker Project, 2017
Córdoba, Argentina

For this artistic exploration of his family home, a former 1940s filling station in the Luque province of Argentina, architect Martin Marro created a living capsule from an old diesel tank that once would have been buried beneath the forecourt. Inside, it is fitted out with a bed, seating, lighting and shelves, and serves as an exhibition space for Marro's drawings of his family home. He describes it as a space to reflect on the hegemony of progress, environmental pollution and the acceleration of productivity processes. Visitors have described it as a place where time stops, as a refuge or escape pod, but also as a warning about the future, including one woman who noted: 'What I understand from this project is that there is little space left on earth, and few truly natural places in harmony and balance. The human being is everywhere and has invaded everything.'⁴⁷

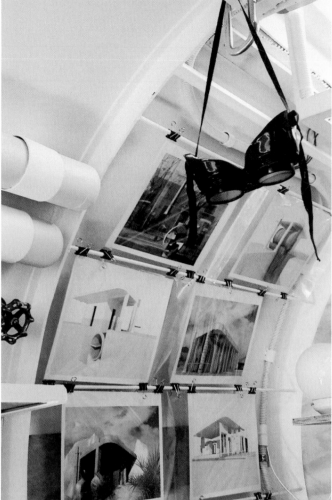

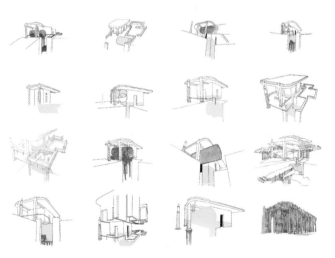

Studio Edward van Vliet
The Yays – Crane Apartment, 2018
Amsterdam, Netherlands

High-end design firm Studio Edward van Vliet has transformed a dilapidated crane into a luxury apartment on Amsterdam's KNSM island, named for the Koninklijke Nederlandsche Stoomboot-Maatschappij (Royal Dutch Steamboat Company). Inside, the space has all the comforts of an exclusive hotel, but outside, its original industrial appearance has been preserved. The crane was built in 1957, and has seen the area shift from a busy dockland to an anarchic squatter camp, and now to a smart residential neighbourhood. The island's former inhabitants improvised homes in and among the derelict buildings with whatever they could find. Van Vliet's design shows how a once fringe activity is becoming a more widespread way of building homes from waste.

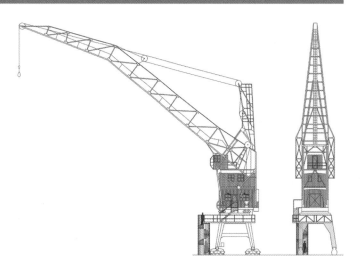

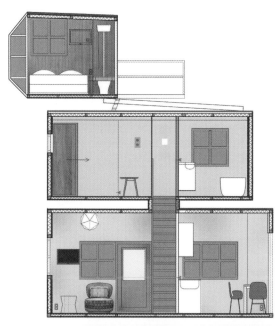

ANYTHING CAN BECOME SOMETHING ELSE

WEAVE

WEAVE
A highrise for bacteria

Like spiders who recognize weaving as a versatile construction method of superb tensile strength, the architects and designers in this chapter also value the structural resilience of woven fibres over static industrial materials, updating the age-old techniques of knitting and weaving through the application of contemporary technologies. Some of the prototypes included here may not look like houses yet, but new research and evolving techniques are producing ecologically sound and flexible models that could make woven homes a practical solution for low-impact living on earth and beyond.

Stéphanie Chalthiel of MuDD Architects combines 3D-knitting technology with water-repellent recycled polyester to produce portable outdoor shelters, or 'knitted pergolas' (p. 236). Architect Bastian Beyer and designer Daniel Suárez take a transdisciplinary approach in projects such as BioKnit (p. 237), placing textiles within an expanded field of building, design and philosophy, experimenting with the structural capabilities of textile systems. Jan Serode's approach sits between energy, design and health. With projects like Smart Skin (p. 239), a polyester façade for buildings that absorbs hazardous nitrogen oxides, he aims to bring concrete-and-glass infrastructure from past decades up to code and avoid CO_2-intensive teardowns.

Impact reduction is behind Warith Zaki and Amir Amzar's Seed of Life colony (p. 238), a connected village on Mars of modular pods made from farmed bamboo for fifty residents. There is also a long tradition of using bamboo to erect dwellings here on Earth, particularly in South America, Africa and South East Asia. For S House (p. 241) in the tropical Mekong River Delta of Vietnam, Vo Trong Nghia combines a lightweight precast concrete frame with woven panels of local nipa palm to create a house with strong structural bones, and the passive-energy benefits of the intertwined palms. Abeer Seikaly also sees the relationships between craft, community and technology with projects like Chrysalis (p. 239), comprising six hyperbolic paraboloid modules, and Weaving A Home (p. 240), a folded skin stretched across pre-stressed radial frames, both of which take their cues from traditional Arab tent architecture.

MuDD Architects
Knitted Pergolas, 2019
Prototype

These portable domes were made using the WholeGarment computerized knitting machine, developed by Spanish manufacturer Shima Seiki, which can knit an item three dimensionally in a single piece, with no seams, greatly reducing material waste. One advantage of 3D-knitting is that it can fabricate complex geometries using integrated structural patterning to generate a series of holes, or pointelle. When transferred to architecture, this means the building has an elastic and responsive skin that expands, contracts and breathes. It also allows for a bespoke solution to any given space. The knitting program can be sent by email to anyone with access to the same machine.

MuDD Architects
D.Lights, 2021
Madrid, Spain

For the 2021 Casa Decor in Madrid, Stéphanie Chaltiel returned to 3D-knitting technology on a much larger scale to produce two lightweight, semi-transparent beige vaults. The fabric has differing patterns, densities and degrees of transparency, and features an integrated LED light system, developed by ProtoPixel, which produces various patterns and colours within its interior. The lights work in sync with a sound program to tell the story of a day and a night in a forest. A sudden evening rain shower causes the lights to flash, and then trickle down like raindrops. With the break of a new day and the chirping of birds, the lights begin to glow. Offering more than just shelter, the space is an experiential atmosphere that stirs the senses. For this small habitat, Chaltiel has also integrated the drone technology used in other projects. Here, the drones buzz back and forth as benevolent construction assistants, resembling worker bees. Their choreographed movements in the air are reflected in changing patterns of light inside. As the drones approach, the lights fluctuate in hue and intensity.

Bastian Beyer and Daniel Suárez
BioKnit, 2019
Prototype

With this project, a column of soft knit has been transformed into a rigid, weight-bearing structure via a biochemical process known as 'bacterially induced calcite precipitation'.[48] Jute fibres were treated with an isolated strain of a non-genetically modified bacteria (also found in everyday soil), along with chloride and urea, triggering a biochemical reaction that forms microscopic calcite bridges between the individual strands, gradually reinforcing them.

The first column could support its own weight, and a newer version – made with in collaboration with Soletanche Bachy in France – far exceeds the structural capabilities of the first. These processes might not yet fit into our current industrial landscape or conventional architecture, notes Beyer, but they demonstrate that interdependent relationships with other micro-habitats are possible.

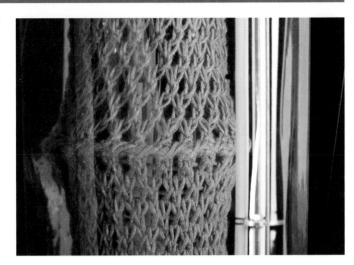

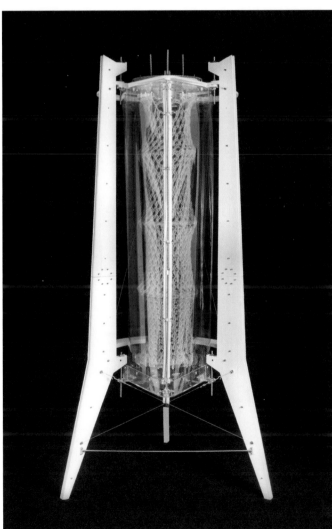

Warith Zaki and Amir Amzar
Seed of Life, 2019
Prototype

Seed of Life is an idea for a habitable colony on the southern hemisphere of Mars, where satellite studies have shown surface ice with the possibility of frozen water beneath. Because the Martian atmosphere is 95 per cent carbon dioxide, it is ideal for growing bamboo at an accelerated rate. Upon reaching its full height, the bamboo is then cut and woven around pressurized environments inflated from capsules used to transport the seedlings. These self-contained spaces are made from ETFE, a fluorine-based, non-corrosive and heat-resistant plastic.

The entire process would be completed within four years, including initial exploration for ice sources, a two-year travel time for the capsules, greenhouse growth and harvesting. As well as construction material, the bamboo could also be used for food.

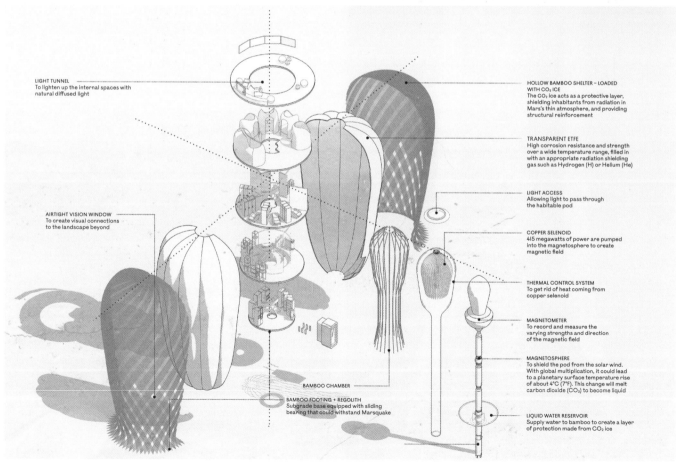

LIGHT TUNNEL
To lighten up the internal spaces with natural diffused light

AIRTIGHT VISION WINDOW
To create visual connections to the landscape beyond

BAMBOO CHAMBER

BAMBOO FOOTING + REGOLITH
Subgrade base equipped with sliding bearing that could withstand Marsquake

HOLLOW BAMBOO SHELTER – LOADED WITH CO₂ ICE
The CO_2 ice acts as a protective layer, shielding inhabitants from radiation in Mars's thin atmosphere, and providing structural reinforcement

TRANSPARENT ETFE
High corrosion resistance and strength over a wide temperature range, filled in with an appropriate radiation shielding gas such as Hydrogen (H) or Helium (He)

LIGHT ACCESS
Allowing light to pass through the habitable pod

COPPER SELENOID
415 megawatts of power are pumped into the magnetosphere to create magnetic field

THERMAL CONTROL SYSTEM
To get rid of heat coming from copper selenoid

MAGNETOMETER
To record and measure the varying strengths and direction of the magnetic field

MAGNETOSPHERE
To shield the pod from the solar wind. With global multiplication, it could lead to a planetary surface temperature rise of about 4°C (7°F). This change will melt carbon dioxide (CO_2) to become liquid

LIQUID WATER RESERVOIR
Supply water to bamboo to create a layer of protection made from CO_2 ice

Jan Serode
Smart Skin Textile Façade, 2020
Prototype

Situated between energy, design and health, Jan Serode's approach stems from the question: 'How can a building envelope perform better?' His polyester façades are coated in nano titanium oxide, and absorb hazardous the nitrogen oxides found in the air (the number-one pollutant in cities), converting them chemically into harmless salts that are then washed away when it rains. The water can be collected and used for fertilizing, and, notes Serode, humans can actually drink what comes off the building.

Abeer Seikaly
Chrysalis, 2015
Prototype

With this project, structure and envelope merge into a 'performative self-structuring building system'.[49] The folds resemble the overlapping scales of a pine cone and help collect, store and transport moisture.

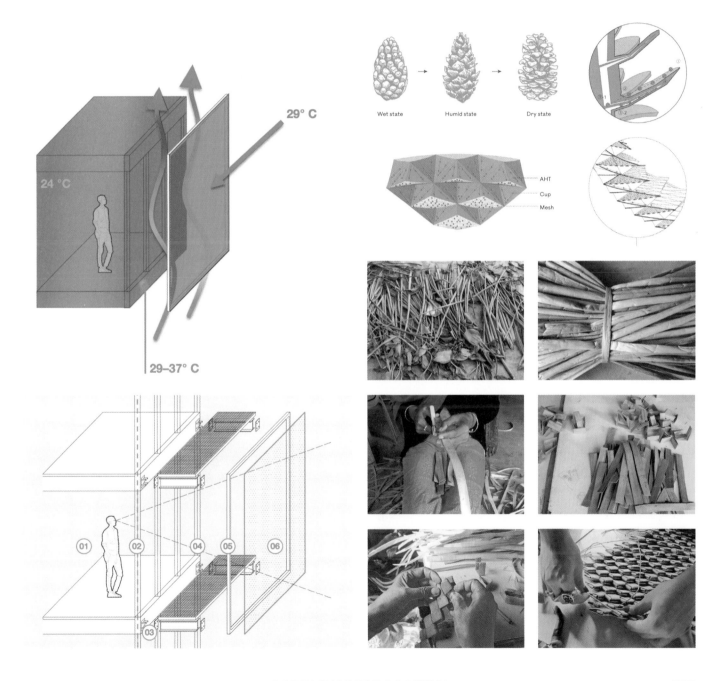

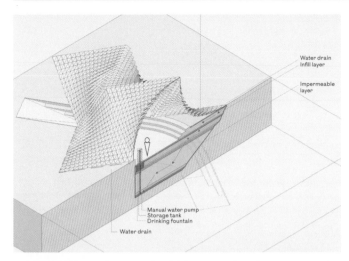

Abeer Seikaly
Weaving a Home, 2013
Prototype

Abeer Seikaly's practice involves observation and field research, together with designing by making. She supports a cradle-to-cradle approach to placemaking and finds valuable resources in the social technologies already present in indigenous societies.

'I really believe in embodied knowledge,' she says. 'It helps you understand and appreciate the world in a much more solid way'.[50]

Seikaly adds that in this age of homelessness, displacement has become the reality for over sixty-five million people, yet refugee camps are isolating, faceless environments that are 'too rigid to accommodate different scales of function'.[51]

Instead of viewing shelter from the perspective of functional design, she approaches it from the belief that all shelter is embedded in the local resources and skills of the community of the place in which it is erected. The eventual by-product is community empowerment.

Vo Trong Nghia Architects
S House, 2014
Long An, Vietnam

Developed for a kidney-bean farmer in the tropical Mekong Delta, this house comprises a lightweight, precast concrete frame clad in woven panels of nipa palm, which is inexpensive, familiar to local residents and in harmony with its surroundings. With the average income for a farmer in the delta at around $100 a month, there is little left for building or maintaining a home. By mass-producing the foundation and frame, the architects have made it possible to drastically lower construction costs while improving the quality and life span of the overall structure. The use of local nipa palm for the exterior enables residents to maintain their homes on a very small budget. The 30 m² (323 sq ft) house can be dismantled and reassembled in a new location and costs only $4,000. The concrete frame and foundation are easily transported to site by boat, and the straightforward bolted assembly encourages residents to participate in the house's construction.

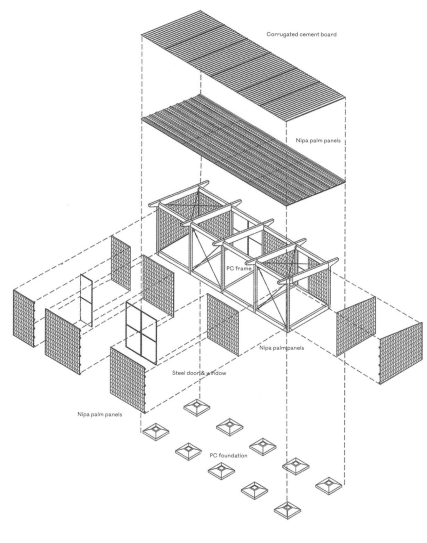

Corrugated cement board

Nipa palm panels

PC frame

Nipa palm panels

Steel door & window

Nipa palm panels

PC foundation

NOTES

1   TRIAS, project description, 27 July 2020.
2   Gartnerfuglen Arkitekter and Mariana de Delás, project description, 7 April 2020.
3   Mary Arnold-Forster Architects, project description, 10 August 2020.
4   EDAA, interview with the authors, 17 April 2020.
5   Aires Mateus, interview with the authors, 15 February 2021.
6   i/thee, written interview with the authors, 25 March 2021.
7   Elemental, project description, 8 August 2020.
8   Ensamble AI, written interview with the authors, 13 April 2020.
9   'Design Build Bluff/This Is Utah,' YouTube, 10 April 2020, https://www.youtube.com/watch?v=8aPNgha-JkE; accessed 26 April 2021.
10 Kofink Schels, written interview with the authors, 21 July 2020.
11 Carlo Ratti Associati, project description.
12 Kéré Architecture, written interview with the authors, 11 May 2020.
13 Marc Thorpe Design, email correspondence with the authors, 28 July 2020.
14 DUST, written interview with the authors, 5 August 2020.
15 Office of Jonathan Tate, written interview with the authors, 30 November 2020.
16 David Burgher, press release, 'New virtual reality device will help improve quality of life for people living with dementia,' https://vr-ep.com/about/; accessed 28 August 2021.
17 Social Bite, project description, https://social-bite.co.uk/the-social-bite-village/, accessed 31 August 2021.
18 Beta, project description, 29 January 2021.
19 Walllasia, project description, 29 July 2020.
20 Pau Hui Kao, Strength from Struggle, PhD diss., Master of Contextual Design, Design Academy Eindhoven, 2016, p. 36.
21 Space Popular, project description, 27 November 2020.
22 Lucy McRae, project description, https://www.lucymcrae.net/compression-carpet, accessed 27 July 2021.
23 Harry Schaeffer, written interview with the authors, 15 July 2020.
24 Yutaka Sho, 'Northern Designers in Africa: A Political Diary of Building a House in Rwanda', 102nd ACSA Annual Meeting Project Proceedings, Globalizing Architecture/Flows and Disruptions, 2014.
25 World Habitat Award Winners, https://world-habitat.org/world-habitat-awards/winners-and-finalists/plastic-bottle-houses-sahrawi-refugees/#resident-stories, accessed 28 August 2019
26 Upcycle Africa, interview with the authors, 1 March 2020.
27 Matthew Butcher, 'A lyrical architecture of the flood: landscape, infrastructure and symbiosis', Arq 19:3 (2015).
28 Mary Mattingly, written interview with the authors, 25 February 2020.
29 Matthew Barnett Howland, project description.
30 Estudio Campana, interview with the authors.
31 Terreform ONE, http://thisisalive.com/fab-tree-hab-village-living-graft-prefab-structure.
32 Dean's Lecture Series 2018, 'Joshua Bolchover and John Lin, Rural Urban Framework: New Contexts,' YouTube, 10 May 2018, https://www.youtube.com/watch?v=a3WkZ5ILDOY; accessed 5 May 2021.
33 Icon, email interview with the authors, 26 March 2021.
34 Ibid.
35 Ibid.
36 SeARCH, email interview with the authors, 28 March 2021.
37 Emerging Objects, project description, http://emergingobjects.com/project/cabin-of-3d-printed-curiosities; accessed 2 June 2021.
38 Press release, 'TECLA – technology and clay', 20 April 2021.
39 WASP, email interview with the authors, 7 May 2021.
40 Ibid.
41 Bjarke Ingels Group, project description, https://big.dk/#projects-mars; accessed 27 March 2021.
42 Bjarke Ingels, 'An architect's guide to living on Mars', Ted Talk, April 2019, https://www.ted.com/talks/bjarke_ingels_an_architect_s_guide_to_living_on_mars; accessed 27 March 2021.
43 Dennis Carter, interview with the authors, 26 November 2020.
44 Proarh, written interview with the authors, 7 July 2021.
45 JYA-Rchitects, project description, 29 August 2020.
46 Refunc, interview with the author, 20 February 2020.
47 Martin Marro, written interview with the author, 6 August 2020.
48 Bastian Beyer and Daniel Suárez, interview with the authors, 1 March 2021, and email correspondence, 29 May 2021.
49 Abeer Seikaly, project description, https://abeerseikaly.com/chrysalis/; accessed 13 April 2021.
50 Abeer Seikaly, interview with the authors, 15 January 2021.
51 Abeer Seikaly, project description, https://abeerseikaly.com/weaving-a-home-2013/; accessed 13 April 2021.

DIRECTORY

Mary Arnold-Forster Architects (30)
Perthshire, Scotland, UK
maryarnold-forster.co.uk

Mary Mattingly (135)
New York, New York, USA
marymattingly.com

Matthew Barnett Howland (142)
Eton, Berkshire, UK
matthewbarnetthowland.com

Matthew Butcher (130, 131)
London, UK
matthewbutcher.org

Mikhail Riches (72)
London, UK
mikhailriches.com

Mobius Architekci (51)
Warsaw, Poland
mobius.pl

MuDD Architects (204, 236)
Barcelona, Spain
muddarchitects.com

MUD Projects (226, 227)
Netherlands
mud-projects.com

Mu Jun (79)
Beijing, China
bucea.edu.cn

NASA Institute for Advanced
Concepts (153)
Mountain View, California, USA
nasa.gov

Neon Saltwater (108)
Seattle, Washington, USA
neonsaltwater.com

Nhlanhla Ndlovu (68)
Soweto, South Africa
hustlenomics.co.za

Nice Architects (160)
Bratislava, Slovakia
niceandwise.sk

Nishizawa Architects (97)
Ho Chi Minh, Vietnam
nishizawaarchitects.com

Nøysom Arkitekter (68)
Oslo, Norway
noysomarkitekter.no

Office of Jonathan Tate (91)
New Orleans, Louisiana, USA
officejt.com

Pao Hui Kao (109)
Eindhoven, Netherlands
paohuikao.com

Patrick Nadeau (165)
Paris, France
patricknadeau.com

People's Architecture Office (171, 172)
Beijing, China
peoples-architecture.com

Philip Beesley Studio (106)
Toronto, Ontario, Canada
philipbeesleyarchitect.com

Phillip K. Smith III (106)
Palm Desert, California, USA
pks3.com

Phooey Architects (194)
Fitzroy North, Victoria, Australia
phooey.com.au

Practice Architecture (143, 145)
London, UK
practicearchitecture.co.uk

Precht (42, 43)
Austria
precht.at

Precious Plastic (197)
Eindhoven, Netherlands
preciousplastic.com

Proarh (205)
Zagreb, Croatia
proarh.hr

Rama Estudio (54, 78)
Quito, Ecuador
ramaestudioec.com

Re Arquitectura (222)
San Jose, Costa Rica
re-arquitectura.com

Redhouse Studio (153)
Cleveland, Ohio, USA
redhousearchitecture.org

Reform Architekt (33)
Lodz, Poland
reformarchitekt.pl

RE4 Project (197)
Brindisi, Italy
re4.eu

Refunc (228)
The Hague, Netherlands
refunc.nl

RicharDavidArchitekti (158)
Prague, Czech Republic
richardavid.cz

Roundhouse Platform (55)
sites.google.com/usc.edu/roundhouse

Rural Urban Framework (163, 164)
Hong Kong, China
rufwork.hku.hk

Rural Urban Synthesis Society (73)
London, UK
theruss.org

SAWA Architecture (92)
London, UK
sawa-architecture.org

SeARCH (50, 182)
Brooklyn, New York, USA
spacexarch.com

Social Bite (93)
Edinburgh, Scotland, UK
social-bite.co.uk

Space&Matter (132)
Amsterdam, Netherlands
spaceandmatter.nl

Space Popular (110)
London, UK
spacepopular.com

SsD Architecture (100)
Seoul, Korea
ssdarchitecture.com

Stefano Boeri Architetti (41)
Milan, Italy
stefanoboeriarchitetti.net

Studio 804 (158)
Lawrence, Kansas, USA
studio804.com

Studio Edward van Vliet (231)
Amsterdam, Netherlands
creatingworlds.edwardvanvliet.com

Studio Kathryn Larsen (206)
Netherlands/Denmark
kathrynlarsen.com

Studio Morison (152)
North Wales, UK
morison.info

Suzuko Yamada Architects (43)
Tokyo, Japan
suzukoyamada.com

Tagarro-de Miguel Arquitectos (174)
Gijón and Oviedo, Spain
tagarrodemiguelarquitectos.es

Taller Hector Barroso (24)
Mexico City, Mexico
tallerhectorbarroso.com

Tateh Lehbib (122)
Tindouf, Algeria
twitter.com/sandships

Tatiana Bilbao Estudio (33)
Mexico City, Mexico
tatianabilbao.com

Tav Group (147)
Haifa, Israel
tavgroup.com

Terreform ONE (150)
Brooklyn, New York, USA
terreform.org

Tomoaki Uno Architects (90)
Nagoya, Japan
unotomoaki.com

TRIAS (25)
Sydney, Australia
trias.com.au

TRS Studio (223)
Lima, Peru
trsworkshop.com

Upcycle Africa (123)
Mpigi, Uganda
upcycleafrica.org

Vandkunsten Architects (206)
Copenhagen, Denmark
vandkunsten.com

Vo Trong Nghia Architects
(38, 39, 40, 241)
Ho Chi Minh, Vietnam
vtnarchitects.net

VUILD (145)
Kanagawa, Japan
vuild.co.jp

Walllasia (101)
Bangkok, Thailand
walllasia.com

WASP (185, 186)
Massa Lombarda, Italy
3dwasp.com

Yakusha Design (107)
Kiev, Ukraine
yakusha.design

ZAV Architects (123)
Tehran, Iran
zavarchitects.com

PROJECT CREDITS

Entre Pinos Housing (24)
Valle de Bravo, Mexico
Taller Hector Barroso, 2017
Area: 1,700 m² (18,299 sq ft)

Slate Cabin (25)
Snowdonia, Wales, UK
TRIAS, 2017
Area: 13 m² (140 sq ft)

Casa Invisible (26)
Ljubljana, Slovenia
Delugan Meissl Associated
Architects, 2013
Area: 50 m² (538 sq ft)

Antoine (28)
Verbier, Switzerland
Bureau and Leopold Banchini, 2014

Gjemmested (30)
Telemark, Norway
Gartnerfuglen Arkitekter
and Mariana de Delás, 2017

An Cala (30)
Sutherland, Scotland, UK
Mary Arnold-Forster Architects, 2019
Area: 100 m² (1,076 sq ft)

The Truffle (31)
Costa da Morte, Spain
Ensamble Studio, 2010
Area: 25 m² (269 sq ft)

Casa Meztitla (32)
Tepoztlán, Mexico
EDAA, 2014
Area: 400 m² (4,306 sq ft)

Los Terrenos (33)
Monterrey, Mexico
Tatiana Bilbao Estudio, 2016
Area: 480 m² (5,167 sq ft)

Izabelin House (33)
Izabelin, Poland
Reform Architekt, 2014
Area: 400 m² (4,306 sq ft)

House for Trees (38)
Ho Chi Minh, Vietnam
Vo Trong Nghia Architects, 2014
Area: 226 m² (2,433 sq ft)
Site area: 474 m² (5,102 sq ft)

Bamboo House (38)
Ho Chi Minh, Vietnam
Vo Trong Nghia Architects, 2016
Area: 217 m² (2,336 sq ft)
Site area: 61 m² (657 sq ft)

Ha House (39)
Ho Chi Minh, Vietnam
Vo Trong Nghia Architects, 2019
Area: 175 m² (1,884 sq ft)
Site area: 137 m² (1,475 sq ft)

Breathing House (40)
Ho Chi Minh, Vietnam
Vo Trong Nghia Architects, 2019
Area: 343 m² (3,692 sq ft)

Vertical Forest (41)
Milan, Italy
Stefano Boeri Architetti, 2014

The Farmhouse (42)
Precht, 2017

Yin and Yang House (43)
Edersee, Germany
Precht, 2017

Daita2019 (43)
Tokyo, Japan
Suzuko Yamada Architects, 2019
Area: 138 m² (1,485 sq ft)

Villa Vals (50)
Vals, Switzerland
SeARCH and Christian Müller
Architects, 2009

House in Monsaraz (51)
Alentejo, Portugal
Aires Mateus, 2018
Area: 174 m² (1,873 sq ft)
Site area: 21,100 m² (227,119 sq ft)

Green Line (51)
Warmia, Poland
Mobius Architekci, 2019
Area: 580 m² (6,243 sq ft)

C'an Terra (52)
Menorca, Spain
Ensamble Studio, 2020
Area: 1,000 m² (10,764 sq ft)

Casa Patios (54)
Lasso, Ecuador
Rama Estudio, 2018

Iceberg Living Station (54)
Antarctica
MAP Architects, 2010

Agg Hab (55)
Clarendon, Texas, USA
i/thee and Roundhouse
Platform, 2020
Area: 37 m² (400 sq ft)

Quinta Monroy (60)
Iquique, Chile
Elemental, 2004
Area: 5,000 m² (53,820 sq ft)
Built area: 3,500 m² (37,674 sq ft)

Villa Verde (60)
Constitución, Chile
Elemental, 2010
Area: 5,688 m² (61,225 sq ft)

**Architectural System for Rural
Social Housing (61)**
Sierra Nevada de Santa
Marta, Colombia
Ensamble AI, 2012
Area: 42 m² (452 sq ft)

Silver Slice (62)
Bluff, Utah, USA
DesignBuildBLUFF, 2019

Badger Springs (62)
Bluff, Utah, USA
DesignBuildBLUFF, 2015

TIA House (63)
Almería, Spain
Kofink Schels, 2016
Area: 65 m² (700 sq ft)

Hustlenomics (68)
Soweto, South Africa
Nhlanhla Ndlovu, 2015

**Svartlamon Experimental
Housing (68)**
Trondheim, Norway
Nøysom Arkitekter, 2017
Area: 350 m² (3,767 sq ft)

Granby Four Streets (69)
Liverpool, UK
Assemble, 2013

**Social Production of Housing:
Exercise I (70)**
Puebla, Mexico
Comunal, 2015
Area: 80 m² (861 sq ft)

**Social Production of Housing:
Exercise II (70)**
Puebla, Mexico
Comunal, 2016

Kenton Women's Village (71)
Portland, Oregon, USA
Center for Public Interest
Design, 2015

Goldsmith Street (72)
Norwich, UK
Mikhail Riches
and Cathy Hawley, 2019

Church Grove (73)
London, UK
Rural Urban Synthesis Society, 2021

Livingboard (73)
Karnataka, India
Carlo Ratti Associati, 2018

Casa Lasso (78)
Lasso, Ecuador
Rama Estudio, 2019
Area: 350 m² (3,767 sq ft)

Building With Earth (79)
Macha, China
Professor Mu Jun and Bridge
to China, ongoing

Gando Teachers' Housing (82)
Gando, Burkina Faso
Kéré Architecture, 2004
Area: 930 m² (10,010 sq ft)

Dakar Houses (83)
Dakar, Senegal
Marc Thorpe Design, ongoing

Rammed-Earth Housing (83)
Accra, Ghana
Hive Earth, ongoing

Tucson Mountain Retreat (85)
Tucson, Arizona, USA
DUST, 2012
Area: 338 m² (3,640 sq ft)

Ogimachi House (90)
Nagoya, Japan
Tomoaki Uno Architects, 2019
Area: 115 m² (1,238 sq ft)

Bastion (91)
New Orleans, Louisiana, USA
Office of Jonathan Tate, 2018
Area: 5,258 m2 (56,600 sq ft)

A House for a Victim (92)
Ntarama, Rwanda
SAWA Architecture, 2015
Area: 70 m² (753 sq ft)

Virtual Reality Empathy Platform (93)
Galashiels, Scotland, UK
David Burgher

Social Bite Village (93)
Edinburgh, Scotland, UK
Social Bite, 2018

Three-Generation House (94)
Amsterdam, Netherlands
Beta, 2018
Area: 450 m² (4,844 sq ft)

Charles House (96)
Melbourne, Victoria, Australia
Austin Maynard Architects, 2017
Area: 348 m² (3,746 sq ft)

House in Chau Doc (97)
Chau Doc, Vietnam
Nishizawa Architects, 2017
Area: 340 m² (3,660 sq ft)

A Guy, a Bulldog, a Vegetable Garden and the Home They Share (98)
Madrid, Spain
Husos Arquitecturas, 2018
Area: 46 m² (495 sq ft)

Songpa Micro-Housing (100)
Seoul, South Korea
SsD Architecture, 2017

Women's Dormitory and Meditation Building (101)
Chonburi Province, Thailand
Walllasia, 2018
Area: 12,000 m² (129,167 sq ft)

Lucid Stead (106)
Joshua Tree, California, USA
Phillip K. Smith III, 2013

Futurium Noosphere (106)
Berlin, Germany
Philip Beesley Studio, 2019

Faina (107)
Kiev, Ukraine
Yakusha Design, 2021

Virtual Rooms (108)
Seattle, Washington, USA
Neon Saltwater, 2019–21

Paper Pleats (109)
Eindhoven, Netherlands
Pao Hui Kao, 2020

The Venn Room (110)
Tallinn, Estonia
Space Popular, 2019

Compression Carpet (113)
Los Angeles, California, USA
Lucy McRae, 2019

Eco-Dome (118)
Hesperia, California, USA
CalEarth, 2003
Area: 37 m² (400 sq ft)

Earth One Vaulted Home (118)
Hesperia, California, USA
CalEarth, 2007
Area: 214 m² (2,300 sq ft)

Homey Dome (120)
Taos, New Mexico, USA
CalEarth and Harry Schaeffer, 2019

Masoro House (121)
Masoro, Rwanda
GA Collaborative, 2013
Area: 86 m² (926 sq ft)

Plastic Bottle Houses (122)
Tindouf, Algeria
Tateh Lehbib, 2017

Round Houses (123)
Mpigi, Uganda
Upcycle Africa, 2015

Presence in Hormuz 2 (123)
Hormuz, Iran
ZAV Architects, 2020
Area: 10,300 m² (110,868 sq ft)

Flood House (130)
Thames Estuary, UK
Matthew Butcher, 2016
flood.house

Silt House (131)
Thames Estuary, UK
Matthew Butcher, 2015

Bang Bang House (131)
Thames Estuary, UK
Matthew Butcher, 2017

Schoonschip (132)
Amsterdam, Netherlands
Space&Matter, 2021
schoonschipamsterdam.org

Urban Rigger (134)
Copenhagen, Denmark
Bjarke Ingels Group, 2016
Area: 680 m² (7,319 sq ft)

Wetland (135)
Philadelphia, Pennsylvania, USA
Mary Mattingly, 2017

Buoyant Ecologies Float Lab (136)
Oakland, California, USA
Architectural Ecologies Lab, 2019

Waterline (136)
Dhangethi, Maldives
Architectural Ecologies Lab, 2020

Cork House (142)
Berkshire, UK
Matthew Barnett Howland, 2019
Area: 75 m² (807 sq ft)

Flat House (143)
Cambridgeshire, UK
Practice Architecture, 2019
Area: 100 m² (1,076 sq ft)

Polyvalent Studio (145)
Cambridgeshire, UK
Practice Architecture, 2019
Area: 30 m² (323 sq ft)

House For Marebito (145)
Nanto, Japan
VUILD, 2019
Area: 52 m² (560 sq ft)

Ashen Cabin (146)
Ithaca, New York, USA
Hannah Design Office, 2019

Zunino House (147)
São Paulo, Brazil
Estudio Campana, 2016

Ein Hod Ecological House (147)
Ein Hod, Israel
Tav Group, 2016
Area: 250 m² (2,691 sq ft)

Fab Tree Hab (150)
Cambridge, Massachusetts, USA
Terreform ONE, 2012

Accretion Project (151)
Kaafu Atoll, Maldives
MAP Architects

Mother ... (152)
Cambridgeshire, UK
Studio Morison, 2020

Mars Habitat (153)
Redhouse Studio and NASA Institute
for Advanced Concepts, 2018

1301 New York Street House (158)
Lawrence, Kansas, USA
Studio 804, 2015

House with a Greenhouse (158)
Hořice, Czech Republic
RicharDavidArchitekti, 2018

Project Ö Cabin (159)
Skjulskäret, Finland
Aleksi Hautamäki and
Milla Selkimäki, 2019
Area: 75 m² (807 sq ft)

Ecocapsule (160)
Bratislava, Slovakia
Nice Architects, 2014
Area: 8.2 m² (88 sq ft)
Internal area: 6.3 m² (68 sq ft)
ecocapsule.sk

Naturbyen (161)
Middelfart, Denmark
Effekt, 2020
Area: 100 m² (1,076 sq ft)

Jintai Village Reconstruction (163)
Bazhong, China
Rural Urban Framework, 2017
Area: 4,000 m² (43,056 sq ft)

A House for All Seasons (164)
Shijiazhuang, China
Rural Urban Framework, 2012
Area: 380 m² (4,090 sq ft)

La Maison-Vague (165)
Reims, France
Patrick Nadeau, 2011
Area: 136 m² (1,464 sq ft)

Concave Roof System (165)
Jiroft, Iran
BMDesign Studios, 2019

Croft Lodge Studio (170)
Herefordshire, UK
Kate Darby Architects and
David Connor Design, 2017
Area: 115 m² (1,238 sq ft)

House No 7 (171)
Isle of Tiree, Scotland, UK
Denizen Works, 2013

Courtyard House Plugin (171)
Beijing, China
People's Architecture Office, 2014
Area: 60 m² (646 sq ft)

Mrs Fan's Plugin House (172)
Beijing, China
People's Architecture Office, 2016

Shangwei Plugin Houses (172)
Shenzhen, China
People's Architecture Office, 2018

Casa Sabugo (174)
Luarca, Spain
Tagarro-de Miguel Arquitectos, 2013

Mr Barrett's House (174)
Geneva, Switzerland
Bureau, 2019
Area: 70 m² (753 sq ft)

Chicon House (180)
Austin, Texas, USA
Icon, 2018
Area: 32 m2 (340 sq ft)

Community First! Village (180)
Austin, Texas, USA
Icon, 2020
Area: house 37 m2 (400 sq ft);
welcome centre 46 m2 (500 sq ft)

New Story Project (181)
Tabasco, Mexico
Icon, 2019
Area: 46 m2 (500 sq ft)

Project Olympus (181)
Prototype
Icon, 2020

Mars X-House VI & V2 (182)
Prototype
SeARCH

Casa Covida (183)
San Luis Valley, Colorado, USA
Emerging Objects, 2020
Area: 14 m2 (150 sq ft)

Cabin of 3D-Printed Curiosities (183)
Oakland, California, USA
Emerging Objects, 2018

TECLA (185)
Massa Lombarda, Italy
WASP, 2021

Gaia House (186)
Massa Lombarda, Italy
WASP, 2018

Mars Science City (187)
Dubai, United Arab Emirates
Bjarke Ingels Group, 2017
Area: 56,810 m2 (611,498 sq ft)

Brighton Waste House (192)
Brighton, East Sussex, UK
BakerBrown, 2014

Up-Cycle House (192)
Blackheath, New South
Wales, Australia
Alexander Symes Architect, 2017
Area: 104 m2 (1,119 sq ft)
Site area: 417 m2 (4,486 sq ft)

Cubo House (194)
Melbourne, Australia
Phooey Architects, 2013
Area: 410 m² (4,413 sq ft)

Useful Waste Initiative (196)
Portland, Oregon, USA
Center for Public Interest
Design, 2016

De Gouverneur (196)
Rotterdam, Netherlands
Architectuur Maken, 2016
Area: 146 m² (1,572 sq ft)

Extruded Plastic Bricks (197)
Eindhoven, Netherlands
Precious Plastic, 2019

Demos (197)
Madrid, Spain; Benevento, Italy;
Toombridge, UK
RE4 Project, 2016–20

Bumpers Oast House (202)
Kent, UK
ACME, 2019

Deer Isle Hostel (203)
Deer Isle, Maine, USA
Dennis Carter and
Anneli Carter-Sundqvist, 2009

Mud Shell (204)
Prototype
MuDD Architects, 2018

Hiža (205)
Kumrovec, Croatia
Proarh, 2015
Area: 230 m2 (2,476 sq ft)
Site area: 3,865 m2 (41,603 sq ft)

The Seaweed Pavilion (206)
Læsø Island, Denmark
Studio Kathryn Larsen, 2019

Modern Seaweed House (206)
Læsø Island, Denmark
Vandkunsten Architects, 2013

Amphibious Houses (212)
Mekong River Delta, Vietnam
Buoyant Foundations Project, 2018

Casa Anfibia (212)
Malacatoya, Nicaragua
Buoyant Foundations Project

Port Maria (213)
Port Maria, Jamaica
Buoyant Foundations Project

Blooming Bamboo Home (213)
Vietnam
H&P Architects, 2013
Area: 44 m² (474 sq ft)

Formosa (216)
Marlow, Buckinghamshire, UK
Baca Architects, 2014
Area: 225 m² (2,422 sq ft)

Othello Way (216)
Stratford-upon-Avon,
Warwickshire, UK
Baca Architects, 2021

The Kentish Classic (217)
London, UK
DHaus, 2018

Containers Franceschi (222)
Santa Ana, Costa Rica
Re Arquitectura, 2017

Low Cost House 2 (223)
Jangheung, South Korea
JYA-Rchitects, 2013
Area: 100 m² (1,076 sq ft)

CN House (223)
Callao, Peru
TRS Studio, 2018

Little Pea (226)
Rotterdam, Netherlands
MUD Projects, 2013
Area: 9 m² (97 sq ft)

Cho (227)
Rotterdam, Netherlands
MUD Projects, 2021

Silo House (228)
The Hague, Netherlands
Refunc, 2013
Area: 13 m² (140 sq ft)

Bunker Project (230)
Córdoba, Argentina
Martin Marro, 2017

The Yays – Crane Apartment (231)
Amsterdam, Netherlands
Studio Edward van Vliet, 2018

Knitted Pergolas (236)
Prototype
MuDD Architects, 2019

D.Lights (236)
Madrid, Spain
MuDD Architects, 2021

Bioknit (237)
Prototype
Bastian Beyer and Daniel Suárez, 2019

Seed of Life (238)
Prototype
Warith Zaki and Amir Amzar, 2019

Smart Skin Textile Façade (239)
Prototype
Jan Serode, 2020

Chrysalis (239)
Prototype
Abeer Seikaly, 2015

Weaving a Home (240)
Prototype
Abeer Seikaly, 2013

S House (241)
Long An, Vietnam
Vo Trong Nghia Architects, 2014

PHOTO CREDITS

All plans and drawings supplied
by the architects
l = left, r = right, t = top, b = bottom,
m = middle

4–5 Gartnerfuglen Arkitekter, Mariana de Delás; 6–7 Rural Urban Framework; 8–9 Tim Crocker; 12–13 Abeer Seikaly; 14–15 David A. Garcia/MAP Architects; 16–17 Effekt; 20 Yoshihiro Koitani; 24 Rory Gardiner Photography; 25 TRIAS Studio (Jonathon Donnelly); 26–7 Christian Brandstätter; 28–9 Dylan Perrenoud; 30l Gartnerfuglen Arkitekter, Mariana de Delás; 30r David Barbour Photography; 31bm, 31br Roland Halbe; 31 (all others) Ensamble Studio; 32 Yoshihiro Koitani; 33l Rory Gardiner Photography; 33r Reform Architekt Group; 34, 38–40 Hiroyuki Oki; 41t Dimitar Harizanov; 41b Boeri; 42, 43l Precht; 43r, 44, 45 Yurika Kono; 46 Neal Lucas Hitch; 50 Photo: Iwan Baan; 51l Nelson Garrido; 51r Przemek Olczyk, Mobius Architekci; 52–3 Ensamble Studio; 54l JAG Studio/Rama Estudio; 54r David A. Garcia/MAP Architects; 55br Sarah Aziz; 55 (all others) Neal Lucas Hitch; 56 David Moreno; 60 Elemental S.A.; 61bl David Moreno; 61tr Juan Pablo Pardo; 61br Simón Fique; 62l Kerri Fukui; 62r DesignBuildBLUFF; 63 Buero Kofink Schels; 64 Nøysom Arkitekter; 68l Hustlenomics; 68tr Nøysom Arkitekter; 68br, 69tl Vigdis Haugtrø; 69ml Markus Lantto and Johanna Gullberg; 69bl Line Anda Dalmar; 69r Assemble/Marie Jacotey; 70 Onnis Luque; 71l Comunal; 71tr NashCO; 71br Zach Putnam; 72 Tim Crocker; 73tl Jon Broome Architects; 73bl Shepheard Epstein Hunter/CGI by Steve Bigg @ ArchitectureFAB; 73r Carlo Ratti Associati; 74 Erik-Jan Ouwerkerk; 78tl Carlos Valarezo; 78 (all others) JAG Studio/Rama Estudio; 79–81 WZQCF; 82 Erik-Jan Ouwerkerk; 83l Marc Thorpe Design; 83r, 84 Joelle Eyeson, Hive Earth; 85 Bill Timmerman; 86 José Hevia/Husos Arquitecturas; 90 Benjamin Hosking; 91t Jackson Hill, courtesy of OJT; 91b William Cocker, courtesy of OJT; 92 SAWA Architecture; 93l David Burgher, Virtual Empathy Platform; 93r, 94l Social Bite Fund; 94r, 95 Ossip van Duivenbode; 96 Peter Bennetts; 97 Nishizawa Architects; 98, 99 José Hevia/Husos Arquitecturas;

100 SsD Architecture; 101 Spaceshift Studio/Pirak Anurakyawachon; 102 Neon Saltwater; 106tl Steve King; 106bl Lance Gerber; 106r Sang Lee; 107 FAINA; 108 Neon Saltwater; 109 Pao Hui Kao/Studio Pao; 110–12 Lara Lesmes and Fredrik Hellberg/Space Popular; 113 Scottie Cameron; 114 Tateh Lehbib and Laroussi Lehbib; 118–19 CalEarth; 120 Harry Schaeffer; 121 GA Collaborative; 122 Tateh Lehbib and Laroussi Lehbib; 123l Upcycle Africa Limited; 123br Payman Barkhordari; 124 DJI; 125l Tahmineh Monzavi; 125tr DJI; 125mr Tahmineh Monzavi; 125br Soroush Majidi; 126 BIG – Bjarke Ingels Group, David Rasmussen; 130 Brotherton-Lock; 131 Matthew Butcher; 132bl, 132br www.isabelnabuurs.nl; 132tr, 132mr, 133 Space&Matter; 134 Urban Rigger, BIG – Bjarke Ingels Group; 135l Laurent de Carniere, BIG – Bjarke Ingels Group; 135r Mary Mattingly; 136tl JD Beltran; 136bl Adam Marcus; 136r, 137 Emma Lou and Cera Ceo; 138 David Grandorge; 142 Matthew Barnett Howland; 143l Magnus Dennis; 143r, 144 Oskar Proctor; 145l David Grandorge; 145r Takumi Ota; 146l HANNAH; 146r Andy Chen; 147l Leonardo Finotti; 147tr Tav Group; 147br, 148–9 Yoav Etiel; 150 Terreform ONE; 151 David A. Garcia/MAP Architects; 152, 153l Charles Emerson, courtesy Studio Morison; 153r Redhouse Studio and NASA Institute for Advanced Concepts; 154 BMDesign Studios; 158l Studio 804, University of Kansas; 158r RicharDavidArchitekti, Jiří Hroník; 159 Aleksi Hautamäki; 160 Ecocapsule; 161, 162 Effekt; 163, 164 Rural Urban Framework; 165l Patrick Nadeau/Hervé Ternisien; 165r BMDesign Studios; 166 James Morris; 170l James Morris; 170tr David Connor; 170mr, 170br James Morris; 171l David Barbour; 171r People's Architecture Office; 172 People's Architecture Office, Gao Tianxia; 173tl, 173ml People's Architecture Office; 173bl, 173r (all) Zhan Changheng; 174l Tagarro-de Miguel Arquitectos – Marián García Mesa; 174r, 175 Dylan Perrenoud; 176 Matthew Millman Photography; 180bl Casey Dunn; 180 (all others) Regan Morton Photography; 181tl, 181bl Joshua Perez; 181tr Bjarke Ingels Group; 182 SeARCH; 183l Elliot Ross,

Emerging Objects; 183r, 184 Matthew Millman Photography; 185, 186 WASP srl; 187 Bjarke Ingels Group; 188, 192l University of Brighton; 192r, 193 Barton Taylor; 194, 195 Peter Bennetts Photographer; 196l Center for Public Interest Design; 196r Ossip van Duivenbode; 197l Precious Plastic; 197tr RE4 Project; 197br ZRS Architekten Ingenieure; 198 Jim Stephenson; 202 ACME; 203l Nick Tsichlis; 203 (all others) courtesy of Deer Isle Hostel; 204 Stéphanie Chaltiel, MuDD Architects; 205t Miljenko Bernfest; 205b Damir Fabijanic; 206l Kelley Hudson; 207 Helene Høyer Mikkelsen for Realdania Byg; 208 DHaus; 212 Buoyant Foundations Project; 214–15 Doan Thanh Ha; 216 Baca Architects; 217 DHaus; 218 Heeman-Fotografie; 222bl Francisco Vasquez May; 222tr Adam Baker; 222mr, 222br Carolina Bello, Pablo Franceschi; 223l Hwang Hyochel; 223r, 224–5 TRS Studio; 226–7 Heeman-Fotografie; 228–9 Refunc.nl; 230 Martin Marro; 231 Studio Edward van Vliet; 232 Warith Zaki, Amir Amzar, Karim Moussa; 236l Stéphanie Chaltiel, MuDD Architects; 236r Imagen Subliminal; 237 Bastian Beyer, Daniel Suárez; 238 Warith Zaki, Amir Amzar, Karim Moussa; 239l Jan Serode; 239r Abeer Seikaly; 240br Tanya Marar; 240 (all others) Abeer Seikaly; 241 Vo Trong Nghia Architects; 242–3 Ensamble Studio; 246–7 Ossip van Duivenbode

ACKNOWLEDGMENTS

We are extremely grateful to all of the architects, designers, researchers and artists who provided us with information and images about their work.

In addition, we would also like to extend a special thanks to the following individuals for their valuable time and support:

Luis Arturo Garcia, EDAA; Antón García-Abril, Ensamble Studio; Héctor Barroso, Taller Héctor Barroso; Manuel Aires Mateus, Aires Mateus e Associados; Christian Müller, gutundgut gmbh, Zürich / gutundgut BV, Rotterdam; David A. Garcia, MAP Architects; Sebastian Kofink, Buero Kofink Schels; Hiroko Yamamoto and Atsushi Yamamoto, DesignBuildBLUFF; Juan Pablo Pardo Vargas and Símon Fique, Ensamble de Arquitectura Integral; Professor Mu Jun, College of Architecture, Beijing University of Civil Engineering and Architecture; Kenny Leung, Wu Zhi Qiao (Bridge to China) Charitable Foundation; Cade Hayes, DUST; Joelle Eyeson, Hive Earth; Francis Kéré, Kéré Architecture; Marc Thorpe, MTD | Marc Thorpe Design; David Burgher, Katherine McKinley, Virtual Reality Empathy Platform Ltd.; Jonathan Tate, Ginny Hanusik, OJT; Edward Dale-Harris, SAWA Architecture; Jinhee Park, SsD architecture + urbanism; Tomoaki Uno, Tomoaki Uno Architects; Philip Beesley, Living Architecture Systems Group/Philip Beesley Studio Inc.; Fredrik Hellberg, Space Popular; Aleksi Hautamäki; Babak M Sadri, BMDesign; Dan Rockhill, Studio 804, School of Architecture, University of Kansas; Friedrich Ludewig, acme; Dennis Carter, Deer Isle Hostel; Kathryn Larsen; Davor Matekovic, Vedrana Jančić, Proarh; Stephanie Chalthiel, MuDD Architects; Heather Peak Morison and Ivan Morison, Studio Morison; Søren Nielsen, Anne-Mette Manelius, Vandkusten; Abeer Seikaly; Bastian Beyer, Research Associate, ArcInTexETN; Jan Serode, Institut für Textiltechnik, RWTH, Aachen University; Joe Evans, Mai Hoan and Vo Trong Nghia, Vo Trong Nghia Architects; Todd Ferry and Julia Mollner, Center for Public Interest Design; Jon Broome; Tateh Lehbib; Kelly Hart; David Monday, Upcycle Africa; Harry Schaeffer; Yutaka Sho and Leighton Beaman, General Architecture Collaborative; Dastan Khalili, CalEarth; Matthew Butcher; Margaret Ikeda, Evan Jones and Adam Marcus, Buoyant Ecologies; Mary Mattingly; Matthew Barnett Howland; James Shen, People's Architecture Office; Kate Darby and David Connor; Cara Caulkins and Dmitri Julius, Icon; Tiziana Teghini and Massimo Moretti, WASP; Rebeccah Pailes-Friedman, SEArch+; Richard Coutts, Baca; Jan Korbes, Refunc; Martin Mario; Boris Duijneveld, MUD Projects; Fernando and Humberto Campana, Silvia Lunazzi, Campana Brothers; Nhlanhla Ndlovu, Hustlenomics; Society of Authors.

It was Lucas Dietrich who first considered our proposal and whose constant enthusiasm and support turned our idea into reality. Thank you, Lucas, for your vision and belief in this book.

We are also grateful to Fleur Jones who guided the project through its initial stages and provided valuable assistance in virtually every detail.

And finally, we thank Elain McAlpine, whose savvy, design expertise and steady editorial hand has shaped this project into a book of wonder, joy and inspiration. We have enjoyed the collaboration immensely.

For our children – Arthur, Harry and Jasper –
who are already guiding us into a healthy future.

And for Tom, who provided everyone who needed
one: a home.

First published in the United Kingdom in 2022 by
Thames & Hudson Ltd, 181A High Holborn, London WC1V 7QX

First published in the United States of America in 2022 by
Thames & Hudson Inc., 500 Fifth Avenue, New York, New York 10110

Houses That Can Save the World © 2022 Thames & Hudson Ltd, London
Text © 2022 Sean Topham and Courtenay Smith

Designed by Daly & Lyon

All Rights Reserved. No part of this publication may be reproduced
or transmitted in any form or by any means, electronic or mechanical,
including photocopy, recording or any other information storage and
retrieval system, without prior permission in writing from the publisher.

British Library Cataloguing-in-Publication Data
A catalogue record for this book is available from the British Library

Library of Congress Control Number 2022931216

ISBN 978-0-500-34371-5

Printed in China by RR Donnelley

MIX
Paper from
responsible sources
FSC® C144853
www.fsc.org

Be the first to know about our new releases,
exclusive content and author events by visiting
thamesandhudson.com
thamesandhudsonusa.com
thamesandhudson.com.au

Courtenay Smith is a freelance curator of contemporary art and design,
whose international exhibitions include *Shanghai Surprise* and the exhibitions
and accompanying books for *Lucy Orta: Body Architecture* and *Xtreme
Houses*. She has held numerous curatorial positions in museums and
galleries in the United States and Germany. Sean Topham has contributed
to various publications, exhibitions and seminars and has written on design
for magazines and newspapers including *The New York Times*, *Dwell*,
The Independent, *The Guardian* and *Icon*.

On the cover: *Front* The Farmhouse (prototype), by Precht (photo: Precht);
Back Slate Cabin, Snowdonia, Wales, by TRIAS (photo: TRIAS Studio/
Jonathon Donnelly)

On pp. 4–5: Gartnerfuglen Arkitekter and Mariana de Delás, Gjemmested,
Telemark, Norway; pp. 6–7: Rural Urban Framework, Jintai Village
Reconstruction, Bazhong, China; pp. 8–9: Mikhail Riches and Cathy Hawley,
Goldsmith Street, Norwich, UK

On pp. 12–13: Abeer Seikaly, Weaving a Home (prototype); 14–15: MAP
Architects, Iceberg Living Station, Antarctica, 16–1:7 Effekt, Naturbyen,
Middelfart, Denmark

On pp. 242–3: Ensamble Studio, C'an Terra, Menorca, Spain; on pp. 244–5
Emerging Objects, Casa Covida, San Luis Valley, Colorado, USA; pp. 246–7:
Beta, Three-Generation House, Amsterdam, Netherlands